LOCH LEVEN and GLENCOE : J. CAMPBELL KERR

D1433349

£2.55

Forsaken Garden

THE gate creaks on rusty hinges,
   As I pass through.
Tall grasses, tangleweed and creeper
   Cover the lovely garden, once I knew.

Pass through the archway, where in
   purple cluster
   Wistaria hung, like grapes upon the
   vine.
A stagnant pool, where water-lilies
   blossomed
   Tangled briar with rose trees intertwine.

A cold wind passes through the garden,
   Rustles the dead leaves on the cold
   apple tree
Mingles with the ghosts of many voices,
   And echoes on my heartstrings
   poignantly.

— Dorothy M. Loughran.

People's Friend Annual

●

CONTENTS

BACK COVER Inverness At Night

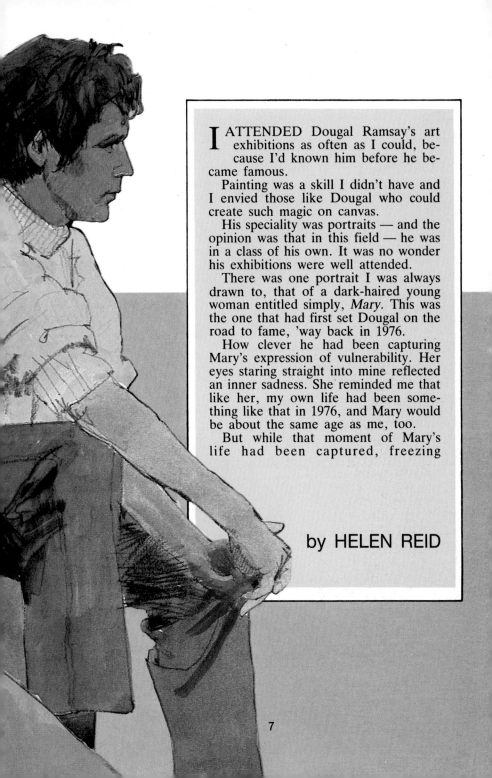

I ATTENDED Dougal Ramsay's art exhibitions as often as I could, because I'd known him before he became famous.

Painting was a skill I didn't have and I envied those like Dougal who could create such magic on canvas.

His speciality was portraits — and the opinion was that in this field — he was in a class of his own. It was no wonder his exhibitions were well attended.

There was one portrait I was always drawn to, that of a dark-haired young woman entitled simply, *Mary*. This was the one that had first set Dougal on the road to fame, 'way back in 1976.

How clever he had been capturing Mary's expression of vulnerability. Her eyes staring straight into mine reflected an inner sadness. She reminded me that like her, my own life had been something like that in 1976, and Mary would be about the same age as me, too.

But while that moment of Mary's life had been captured, freezing

by HELEN REID

7

her for ever in time, the life of Joanna Barnes had moved on ten years, leaving her almost breathless.

Can I really be thirty-five years old, I asked myself. Why, it only seems like yesterday when all my uncertainties about the future began. I closed my eyes and the years just slipped away . . .

★　　　★　　　★　　　★

Though our church was small, it had a very enthusiastic congregation who threw themselves into all the various activities.

Jumble sales were my favourite. I loved the tension of waiting for the doors to open, then the frenzied activity as the crowds thronged in.

Kay Grant, one of the organisers, approached me just before the sale began.

"A quick word, Joanna. Would you be interested in this landscape painting? You said you were looking for one for your flat."

"Rowanbrae!" I gasped. "Thanks, Kay, it's ideal. Rowanbrae's one of my favourite beauty spots. All right if I pay you later, there isn't much time?"

If only I'd had time to take it to the cloakroom, I might have been saved a lot of trouble. But with the sale beginning I only had time to tuck it under the table which served as a counter for the bric-à-brac stall.

The next hour was frantic — the church hall needed elastic sides to hold all the people pushing and shoving. But it was all good-natured and I was glad at last of a breathing space. I was about to grab a quick cup of coffee when I looked up to see a young man holding my painting.

"That's mine," I said politely. "It was laid aside before the sale started."

He looked at Deborah Walker, who was serving him.

"This young lady didn't say anything."

"She didn't know."

"It hasn't got your name on it," he said coolly.

"There wasn't time . . ."

"Have you paid for it?" he demanded.

"No."

"Well, I have. I think that gives me first claim."

With that he turned and walked away, *my* painting under his arm.

Debbie was very apologetic. "Sorry, Joanna, but everything's in such a mess underneath."

I said it was my fault. "I should have moved it to a safe place."

I joined Kay Grant for that welcome cup of coffee behind the scenes.

"It's not so much the painting that rankles but his lack of manners," I said to her as I finished relating the story.

"D'you know who he was?" Kay asked.

"Never seen him before, and I hope not to again."

Kay did her best to smooth my ruffled feathers in her usual

humorous way. "I find it amusing to think of two people arguing over a painting as if it's a priceless work of art. I know the artist and he turns these about by the dozen.

"Dougal Ramsay is a new near neighbour of ours. If you like I'll give you his address, I'm sure he'll have another Rowanbrae for you."

I thanked Kay, saying that I might call on him sometime.

"I didn't want to get steamed up over a painting but I've been rather on edge since Mr Hamilton died."

"Yes, he'll be sorely missed," Kay said with a deep sigh. "A real kenspeckle figure in the town was Tom Hamilton. Many a good blether we've had over the counter of The Coffee Mill. You'll be carrying on as manageress, will you?"

"That depends on what plans Mr Hamilton's nephew has for the shop — after all, it's been left to him."

"Well, it's such a flourishing business, he'd be a fool to make too many changes. The shop may appear old fashioned, but it makes the customers feel comfortable. I wonder if the nephew will be out of the same mould as Tom."

"I've no idea, Kay, I've never met him."

E VER since Tom Hamilton died I'd been plagued with uncertainty about the future. At such times I tended to look back, which was why I'd so much wanted that painting of Rowanbrae.

I hadn't intended to do anything about it immediately but when I returned to my flat that blank space above the mantelpiece caught my eye. I made up my mind to call on this Dougal Ramsay, hoping that he wouldn't mind me bothering him.

Next morning I stood nervously on his doorstep, not sure what kind of greeting to expect or the person. Imagine my surprise therefore when a shaggy beard with face on top appeared at an open window above.

"You're not selling anything, are you?" he shouted down.

"Actually, I came to see you about a painting."

"Then you've come to the right place." He grinned. "If you don't mind I won't come down, I'm covered in paint. Make your way upstairs, my studio's first on the right."

"Thanks."

At least I'm welcome, I thought with a sigh of relief.

"You're a pleasant surprise on a Sunday morning." He smiled when I pushed open the door of his bright airy studio. "I'm Dougal Ramsay. Come in, please."

"Joanna Barnes."

Dougal laughed. "I hope I didn't scare you poking my head out the window. My beard has that effect on people. It's a disguise, you see, I'm hiding from my creditors."

I was liking Dougal Ramsay already. There was a magnetism about his personality which I found most pleasing.

"You said something about a painting, Joanna?"

"A neighbour of yours, Kay Grant, said you might help. I'm looking for a painting of Rowanbrae."

"No bother." He smiled, pulling out a pile of canvases. "Here you are, Rowanbrae from the south, north, east, west — the choice is yours."

I found one which pleased me more than the one I'd lost, and related the story to Dougal.

His eyes twinkled. "I'm flattered that you should think one of my paintings was worth fighting over, so you can have that with my compliments."

"You're very kind, but . . ."

"No buts, Joanna," he said. "You've brightened my Sunday morning, and I've *hundreds* of landscapes — bread and butter stuff to me. My real interest is in portraits, but I'm not doing too well. Have a look at these, they're dreadful, no life, no inspiration.

"If you knew the time I spend with my subjects before I even touch a drop of paint. I make sketches, I photograph them from every angle, we talk because I like to know the person behind the face. Maybe it's because I haven't yet found a subject with whom I'm in complete sympathy."

He smiled again. "Less about me and something about you, Joanna. Where d'you work?"

"Hamilton's in the High Street."

"Of course, The Coffee Mill," Dougal replied. "Marvellous place, the aroma of coffee beans and a marvellous selection of teas."

"Yes, Mr Hamilton was very particular about the brands he bought. Did you know he died recently?"

"I saw it in the paper."

"I've worked for him for nine years, and I'm not particularly looking forward to his nephew taking over. You know what they say about 'new brooms.' "

"Cheer up," Dougal said reassuringly. "He might not be as bad as you think."

He smiled. "Anyway, if he is, come to me and you can cry on my shoulder."

"Thanks, Dougal, you've been very kind."

I left his studio, my heart taking wings, and that feeling lasted all day.

MONDAY morning brought me back to earth with a crash when I was confronted by Gerald Hamilton — Tom's nephew.

If he remembered our words at the jumble sale over the picture, it wasn't mentioned. Only a faint glimmer of recognition showed in his eyes.

"Miss Barnes?"

"Yes."

"I'm Gerald Hamilton."

He transferred his gaze to the shop. "I really don't know why Uncle Tom left me this place, we were never very close."

"Loyalty to his customers and family," I replied. "He wanted The Coffee Mill to continue as before under the Hamilton name."

"But he knew I'm an accountant. I can't keep commuting from Carlisle every day."

"Don't worry about that, I can manage the place when you're not here. I did the same for your uncle."

"Yes, he did say he thought the world of you."

Gerald Hamilton wandered about the shop with a disapproving expression. "Well if the Mill is going to be mine I'd better make the most of it. Come to think of it the place could be quite a profitable sideline for me with some modernisation."

"But you can't!" I exclaimed, horrified.

"My dear Miss Barnes, the shop is just too old fashioned."

"I disagree. It may seem old fashioned to you but that's its strength, the customers get a feeling of security in a world which is changing too fast."

"I notice my uncle's taught you well," Gerald. said with a barely-forced smile.

"He was a wise man."

"But not a rich one," Gerald countered. "And he could have been if he hadn't allowed sentiment to intrude into business sense."

"Money meant little to him," I replied hotly. "Loyalty and service to the community came first."

"We all have our own ideas," Gerald said dismissively. "Now as we'll be working together from time to time, perhaps we should get to know each other better. I'm staying in the Royal Hotel. How about dinner this evening?"

"Sorry, Mr Hamilton. I have a previous engagement."

"Another time then," he said casually. "I'll be staying around for a few days."

He left the Mill, leaving me there trembling with anger. And that was how Dougal Ramsay found me.

"I come in for some coffee and find you in a state of shock. What's happened?"

"Gerald Hamilton happened. That's what!"

"The nephew, I suppose?"·

"Yes."

"And he's bad news?"

"You could say that," I said grimly.

"Come and have lunch with me and tell me all about him."

Eagerly I followed his suggestion, but could hardly eat for my anger.

The Homemaker

DON'T say: "I'm just a housewife,"
   And make it sound so dull,
Of all the people on this earth,
   You live life to the full.
Just think of home and family,
   Without your presence there,
The gap you'd leave I'm sure
   Would drive all to despair.

Walk tall, and know you're truly
   Worth your weight in gold.
The all-embracing love you give,
   Returns a thousandfold.
                  — Georgina Hall.

"How could he walk in like that and casually talk of destroying all his uncle worked for?" I seethed. "Then he had the cheek to casually ask me out to dinner, softening me up no doubt to fall in with his plans. Well, I don't want anything to do with it. I'd rather hand in my notice first."

"And then what?" Dougal said. "You'd be unemployed and Gerald Hamilton would go ahead, anyway, without you. All you'd feel was guilt that you'd let Tom Hamilton down. He may have passed on but it seems he needs your loyalty more than ever.

"Look, Joanna, stay on. That way you can at least be in a position to talk Gerald out of the worst excesses of modernisation plans. Who knows, one of these days you might find the man's human after all?"

Dougal grinned. "Remember, we've something to thank him for. If he hadn't bought your Rowanbrae we wouldn't have met — and that would have been terrible. I mean, look how we're getting on already and we haven't known each other very long."

I laughed. "Oh, Dougal Ramsay, you're proving good for my ego."

"That's working both ways," he replied, then asked hesitantly, "Joanna, I was wondering whether you'd let me paint a portrait of you?"

"Dougal, you're joking!" I exclaimed. "I'm just ordinary, why bother with me?"

"No, Joanna," he said eagerly. "There's a sympathy between us, I can feel it. And you have an inner sadness at the moment which gives your face added beauty. Please, please, this is very important to me."

"Then how can I resist such flattery?" I smiled.

"We'll start straightaway. Say this evening?"

"Yes, all right."

I FOUND sitting for Dougal a wonderful release from the pressures of the shop. Those evenings I spent in his studio were such a happy time for both of us. Dougal was relaxing, too, and because of this seemed to be painting with a new enjoyment and authority.

Naturally he wouldn't let me see the unfinished work, — even although I was burning with impatience.

"I don't need you for any more sittings, but I've quite a lot of work still to do on your painting yet," he told me some time later. "I suggest you go away and forget me for while."

"Can't I come round in the evenings and keep you company while you paint?"

"No, Joanna, I prefer to work alone at this stage."

"All right," I said disappointedly.

I hated the thought of not having Dougal to talk to each evening after a day in the Mill with Gerald. Dougal was like an anchor I could cling to in a sea of uncertainty.

Despite what Gerald had said about leaving the running of the Mill to me, he kept coming back, asking questions, probing into all aspects of the business, even serving behind the counter.

Gradually I found myself handling him quite competently because of the added self-confidence my friendship with Dougal had given me.

I took every chance to tactfully play down his modernisation ideas. Gerald listened carefully but said little which heartened me. Could he be having second thoughts, I wondered.

Then I realised that all his questions had nothing to do with an ulterior motive, he was beginning to take a genuine interest in the work.

Even his suggestion of a new bookkeeping system was put to me as a thought rather than a command.

"I realise you might find it a little tricky at first, but I'll give you all the help I can. Uncle Tom's method was rather haphazard, and as an accountant that rather offends my eye."

"All right." I smiled.

Then he took me completely by surprise.

"I've given you a rough time since I came here and I'm sorry. You see, I've never understood why Uncle Tom left The Coffee Mill to a disinterested nephew who wasn't even close to him. That's why I was so resentful.

"I know how much my uncle loved this place — my modernisation plans were a spiteful attempt to hit back at him."

Gerald smiled ruefully.

"Now I understand why he loved the place and why the customers are so faithful. So many of them have said that there's no place quite like it for service and friendliness. They hope it won't change because I'm the new owner."

He smiled. "I did my best not to be a 'chip off the old block' but maybe I'm more like Uncle Tom than I thought. So they can rest assured the place will still be the same as before. If you'll give me the same loyalty as you gave Uncle Tom?"

"That goes without saying, Gerald."

"Speak-Up, Sammy!"

I'M a budgie called Sammy, and
  here's what I do —
I whistle and sing, and talk the day
  through!
But sometimes, you know, I'm as quiet
  as can be,
When Missy invites all her friends
  in to tea.
They're all very eager and want me
  to sing,
'Cos Missy says, "Sammy's a clever
  old thing!"
It's natural, really, that she should
  be proud,
But I keep my beak shut when there's
  such a large crowd.
And though I am offered a tit-bit
  or two,
And they all keep on saying,
  "Speak-up — Sammy, do!"
I think I will wait 'till they've all
  gone away,
For I've learned such a lot of new
  words today!

— Elizabeth Gozney.

He smiled. "I've learned a lot about loyalty since I came. In fact, I'm beginning to wonder if my uncle left the The Coffee Mill to teach me just that."

I admired Gerald Hamilton from that moment on; to admit such a thing must have been a dent to his pride.

"And one thing more," he said. "About the painting at the jumble sale, that was rude and unforgivable, if you want it back . . ."

"Thanks, but that won't be necessary, I found another one."

And a lot more besides, I told myself, when Dougal phoned to say my portrait was ready for unveiling and asked me if I could call round that evening to see it.

THE moment I arrived at the house I walked up the stairs with Dougal, pouring out the story of my understanding with Gerald.

Dougal was pleased for me.

"I told you not to go by first impressions." And like an excited schoolboy he uncovered my portrait.

"My impression of you," he said proudly.

For a few minutes I stood speechless, before Dougal laughingly asked if I'd lost my tongue.

"Oh, Dougal, it's wonderful, and yet to see my own likeness, to see such beauty when I feel so unbeautiful and ordinary . . . it makes me feel rather a fraud."

"But you are beautiful and very special. Since I first met you my life's never been quite the same. You've given me added strength, there's a new depth and texture to my painting.

"And you're not wearing that look of sadness any more. You're happy now."

"Yes, I am. Oh, Dougal," I whispered, tears misting my eyes.

"Don't be uspet," he said helplessly handing me a hankie.

I laughed through my tears. "A lot you know about women, Dougal Ramsay. These are tears of happiness."

Suddenly we were both laughing and in each other's arms. Dougal held me close and said, "There's no going back now, is there?"

"I don't think I want to," I replied. "Goodness, I can't believe that all this is happening to ordinary Mary Joanna Barnes."

"Mary?"

"My first name. You see, there were four other Marys in my class at school so the teachers called me Joanna. I became so used to being called by my middle name that I've used it ever since."

★　　　★　　　★　　　★

A questioning voice in the art gallery was enough to break into my reminiscing.

"Mary," the lady said to her friend as they glanced intently at the portrait. "What an attractive young woman. I wonder who she was."

"Oh, the artist's wife," I said impulsively.

The women thanked me for the information and moved on to the next painting.

Then Dougal was pushing his way through the crowd towards me. His clothes were smart now, hair and beard neatly trimmed as befitting a famous artist.

"They never even recognised me," I said in mock indignation. "Would you believe it?"

"We're ten years on." Dougal smiled.

"But they did say I was an attractive young woman," I added in some triumph.

"You still are attractive — even more so," came my husband's compliment.

Dougal took a last glance at my portrait.

"You've been a double blessing, you helped to make me famous, and you've made me the happiest man in the world. No-one could ask more from life than that. Let's go home, shall we?" He smiled at me.

My heart was full. Though Mary's name was on the picture, Joanna was the one Dougal loved, and as far as I was concerned, that was all that mattered. ☐

they were first...

THERE can be few of us who, at some time or another, haven't enjoyed a Walt Disney film. Some sixty years ago, he was the first to introduce sound into cartoons and followed this success by making "Flowers And Trees," the first colour cartoon. Many of his later films became household favourites and he and the studio he ran diversified, adding nature films to those wonderful cartoons.

Today fantastic theme parks are a lasting tribute to this giant of the entertainment industry.

MUMMY, can I go out to play?" Raymond Ogilvie nuzzled himself into his mother's side as he spoke.

She was at the sink, supposed to be washing the dishes, only she wasn't. Her hands were in the soapy water but she was just standing still, looking out into the garden.

Raymond guessed that she was staring at the tree again. He wanted to promise her that he wouldn't climb the tree. He wouldn't fall and get taken to the hospital like William. The thought of William, his twin brother, made Raymond feel sad.

He wanted to remind his mother that William was getting better, he'd soon be home from the hospital. But Raymond sensed that his mother wouldn't be listening to him.

He nudged her elbow now with his head as he begged.

"*Please*, Mummy, let me go out and play!"

Leaning against her, he knew that this time she had heard him, because suddenly her side went rigid and cold.

Time To Let Go

by GRACE MACAULAY

He took a step away from her and looked up into her face. But she did not look at him.

She began to wash the dishes at record speed, splashing water and soapy bubbles all over him as she spoke.

"Darling, I've told you — wash your face and hands and comb your hair." And half turning she smiled. "We are all going to Granny's. You like going on the bus, don't you?"

Raymond stared up at her solemnly. She wasn't smiling at him at all. Her smile was going over his head. And it wasn't a proper smile.

He knew that — but he didn't know how he knew. But one thing he did know for a fact — and that was that she wasn't letting him out to play.

16

He turned away, her voice following him as he went upstairs. She doesn't love me any more, he thought, and that's a fact.

Raymond was eight and a half years old. He knew what was a fact. He'd asked his granny, because she often said something and added in a loud voice, nodding her head up and down:

"And that's a fact."

When Raymond asked her what it meant, she'd told him.

"If you know something is definitely true — and nobody can argue about it — then it's a fact."

Raymond liked the phrase. He thought about it a lot and he had put it in his day book at school.

B

It is raining today and that is a fact, he had written.

And the teacher had smiled at him and put a silver star on his work. Then she had touched his eyebrows.

"Frowning won't get you a gold star, Raymond Ogilvie," she said. "But maybe more work would. One sentence is not enough to write in your day book, and you know it."

But what could he write about? If he got out to play there would be lots to write. But he couldn't write the same thing every day . . .

Last night we all went on the bus to my granny's and we had to behave and watch television because there is no room to move about in my granny's house.

He had written something like that three times last week. He sighed sombrely as he reached the top of the stairs.

On the landing outside the bathroom, his little brother, Daniel, said to him:

"What are you crying for, Raymond?"

"I'm *not* crying!" Raymond's shout exploded from his mouth and he tried to push past Daniel.

Then they were both sprawling on the floor, and Mandy, his big sister, was shouting while she pulled them apart, and Greg, his big brother, came to help.

D OWNSTAIRS Julie Ogilvie heard all the commotion but she did nothing about it. Better to let their spirits go just now, she thought, since they'd all have to be quiet later.

Soon they were all organised to go out and Julie Ogilvie marshalled them along to the bus stop. Thankfully, there were no roads to cross.

Once they were safely on the bus, she relaxed slightly. The evening routine was under way.

She would escort the children up to her mother's flat then catch the next bus to the hospital where she would spend an hour alone with William. Then Harry, her husband, would join her, straight from work, and they would both stay with William until he was sleepy.

Soon William will be coming home from hospital, she thought, and I'll be able to look after him myself. We shall all be secure again, under one roof.

She glanced at four-year-old Daniel who was sitting beside her. Then her eyes moved to the three squeezed into the seat in front.

Mandy was going on fourteen. She was starting to want to go out to discos. Greg, at twelve, was a big boy for his age and he had been picked for the school football team. He was looking forward to going to secondary school. But his mother dreaded the thought . . .

Julie Ogilvie's heart seemed to lurch as a wailing voice inside her own head began to ask . . . Why did I have so many children? Why did I ever want a big family? What made me think I could care for so many?

It's just not possible to look after all of them properly, her inner voice protested. We're not short of money — Harry earns a good salary — and I would willingly work day and night to feed and clothe them and keep them clean.

But that's not enough. Children deserve more than that.

Greg was standing up. It was time to get off the bus. She clutched little Daniel's hand fiercely as she warned the others:

"Hold on tightly now. Wait until the bus stops."

A few minutes later, as she left the children with her mother, Julie turned from the door.

"You look tired, Mother," and with an oddly-guilty feeling, she promised, "I'll try to collect them a bit earlier tonight."

"Don't bother about me," her mother answered promptly. "We must all rally round in a crisis." And then with a sympathetic smile, the older woman added:

"Give William my love. I know he doesn't remember me but tell him all the same."

"I will," Julie replied. "I'll show him your photo while I'm telling him."

When Julie arrived at the ward doors, she paused for a moment or two to watch her small son. He was laughing as he tried to play a game of tag with two children who were hopping on crutches.

William had a walking frame, similar to the walking pen he'd had when he was a baby.

Raymond, his twin brother, had loved his walking pen. He would have toddled around all day in it. But William, the more assertive of the two, had always managed to capsize his pen so that he could crawl around under his own steam.

Would he ever be the same again, she wondered.

"He has every chance of making a full recovery," the doctor had said, "but it will take time."

WILLIAM had been unconscious for three days after he tumbled out of the tree house he had built . . . now he was lucky to be alive. But he had to learn all over again how to walk and talk . . .

"Ma . . . ma . . . ," he said, when he saw her.

Julie bent to kiss him. It was lovely that he had begun to recognise her. She wanted to lift him up and hug him and never let him go. But

Grey Magic

THE mountain road is hidden in the grey,
Soft magic that is this season's lovely whim,
To hide the leanness of the earth today,
The poor gaunt trees have veiled each naked limb.

Upon the grass lie opals, you may shake
Great glittering diamonds from the thistle's hair,
And on the leaves the falling raindrops make
A pearly music on the quiet air.
— *Kathleen Wardle.*

that wouldn't help him to get better. So she restrained herself.

She must encourage him to walk and keep talking to him so that he could copy her words.

Harry arrived at half-past six and she told William.

"Here's your daddy, say hello to your daddy."

But at the same time, Julie was aware of a pang of dismay when she took in her husband's weary face. She had never known him to look so tired and drawn.

She wanted to reach out to him and reassure him. Then the moment was gone, for Harry's features were lighting up as William greeted him happily.

"Daddy!" William said the word clearly and lifted his arms up as if he knew that Harry would swing him up into the air and cuddle him.

"You are coming on a treat, aren't you?" Harry's smile included Julie, and he asked William, "Where's your mummy?"

Then there was the ritual of looking at all the family photographs pinned up behind William's bed.

Tonight, William made a good attempt at saying all the names. And when it was time for his parents to go, he smiled as he repeated:

" 'Night, 'night."

"I'll see you in the morning," Julie said softly.

The moment of leaving him was always emotional and her eyes were misty as she said good night to the nurses.

"I believe his progress will be faster than the doctors imagine," Harry said happily as they walked down the steps outside.

"Don't you think . . . ?" he started to say just as Julie lost her footing and he reached out swiftly to catch her before she fell.

"Are you all right?" His voice was filled with alarm as he held on to her. "Are you hurt?"

"No —" Julie said, and immediately became aware of a pain in her ankle.

She was glad to lean against Harry as they slowly descended the remaining steps.

"Have you twisted your ankle again?" Panic was now in Harry's tone as he supported most of her weight.

"What do you mean — *again*?" Julie asked irritably, "I don't make a habit of twisting my ankle."

"You used to when you wore those ridiculous stiletto heels!" Harry said accusingly. "You never would take a telling."

SUDDENLY, for no reason at all Julie giggled and hid her face against his jacket.

"It's no laughing matter!" Harry fumed. "You women have no sense when it comes to fashion."

"Stop it, Harry," she pleaded, "or I shall have hysterics!"

When he stared at her reproachfully, she said good humouredly, "Will you please look at my feet and tell me if I'm wearing flat-heeled shoes or if we've suddenly gone back twenty years in time?"

Harry had the grace to apologise and he confessed:

"I just can't bear the thought of anything happening to you." Gingerly she tried her weight on her ankle.

"How is it?" he asked anxiously.

"Fine," Julie answered. "I don't think I've sprained it — I only lost my balance for a second — then you caught me."

"But not quite soon enough." Harry spoke sombrely. "I should have been holding on to you."

Julie made no reply and they walked silently towards the car park. But thoughts and emotions were spinning around inside her.

She sounded slightly breathless as she put her seat belt on and turned to her husband.

"Harry, that was a silly little accident," she said urgently.

His profile was bleak.

"But it could have been serious." Harry dragged on his own seat-belt and clicked it into place. "Is it painful — should we go back to the casualty department?" he added.

"No, no, truly I'm all right," she said quietly, but as he reached to switch on the ignition, she reached out to stop him.

"Wait, Harry, wait a minute."

Gathering her thoughts into some sort of order, she continued. "Listen, Harry — I feel as if your reaction was like some sort of pattern. I slipped, you panicked, then you were angry, then you blamed yourself — as if my carelessness could possibly be your fault."

Harry listened and watched her face.

Pictures On The Wall

A FUSSY, floral paper
  With leaves of shaded green,
And sprays of climbing roses
  With lilies in between;
A quaint, old-fashioned paper,
  Quite shabby, I'm afraid —
But what enchanting pictures
  Its faded patterns made!

Sometimes, the leaves were islands,
  Remote and bare of trees —
The lilies ghostly galleons
  Afloat on misty seas.
The roses all had faces —
  A cavalier, a clown,
And pretty girls in bonnets
  Dressed up to go to town.

Sometimes, a dragon's cavern
  Appeared among the leaves,
Or Sleeping Beauty's castle,
  With cobwebs round the eaves.
So many magic places
  Were in that paper shown —
So many friendly faces,
  One never felt alone . . .

But they said, "It's outdated,
  It really *has* to go!
A Georgian stripe's the fashion."
  They simply did not know
How many childhood fancies
  Were lost beyond recall
The day they changed the paper
  On the smallest bedroom wall.
    — *Brenda G. Macrow.*

21

"What are you getting at, Julie?" he asked. "I don't understand what you mean."

"Neither do I," Julie admitted, "but I have the feeling — from the way you held me so tightly and helped me into the car — that your next sensation was fear and a great need to protect me."

Before he could comment, she went on, "That's how we have reacted to William's accident."

"I should have had those lower branches cut off the tree," Harry said gloomily. "I blame myself —"

"But William would probably have got the ladder out of the shed," Julie argued. "I've been blaming myself, too, Harry," she added.

"In fact, I've got past the blame stage, although I couldn't forgive myself. But I keep getting dizzy with terror in case anything else happens . . . I want to wrap you and the children in cotton-wool and keep you beside me all the time.

"I won't trust anyone but my own mother to look after them." Julie's voice came to a trembling halt and she stared unseeingly through the car's windscreen.

AFTER a long silence, Harry sighed.

"The other night, when your mother suggested minding the children at our house, my heart nearly stopped," he said. "I was so relieved when you told her you'd bring them to her flat."

"And she nodded — as if she'd been expecting me to say exactly that," Julie said, "as if she knew we needed a bit more time to come to terms with William's accident."

She paused before she continued positively.

"Because that's what it was, Harry — an *accident*. And we must try to put it behind us now."

Straining against the seat belt, Harry leaned across to kiss her, and as they gazed at each other, each of them knew that the days ahead might be difficult — it would be hard to let go of the fears they had been clutching on to.

★   ★   ★   ★

Raymond Ogilvie knew nothing of the discussion which had taken place in the hospital car park. But two days later, he wrote in his school book.

Last night my granny came to our house for tea and then she watched television. My mummy said I could go out to play and I had great fun racing up and down the path on my scooter.

I had a bath, and crisps and orange juice for my supper. When I was in bed my mummy tucked me in and listened to my prayers.

Raymond paused to read over what he had written. Then he chewed the end of his pencil for a while before he carefully added one last sentence.

My mummy loves me and that's a fact.

Somehow, he was sure that the teacher would give him a gold star today. □

Her Birthday Surprise

by SHEILA PEARL

MARGARET screwed up her eyes, still heavy with a night's sleep, to read once more Bob's card on her bedside table.

Happy Birthday, darling! Your loving husband, Bob.

It was the first time since their marriage that he hadn't been lying beside her on her birthday morning. Such a shame he had to be away because of a business trip.

The sitting-room downstairs was filled with the wonderful flowers he had sent the previous day. Margaret didn't like fresh flowers in the bedroom, but Bob's card close by was comforting.

"We'll celebrate when I get back, Margaret," he had said. "A candlelit dinner for two, eh?"

"I'm going to be forty-nine — not twenty-five. Remember? I'll soon be an old lady!" Margaret had replied.

"You could have fooled me," he joked. "But you won't be on your own for your birthday, love, will you? The children will be coming back home here in the evening?"

"I hope so. They've all said they would try to make it. Children! How can you still call them that when there isn't one under twenty years old!"

Margaret handed Bob the carefully-ironed shirts to add to his suitcase.

"But none of them could give me a definite yes or no," she continued. "You know how busy they always seem to be . . . their jobs, their friends . . ."

Margaret sighed. "It was so much easier when they were little. I sometimes feel embarrassed asking them to come home nowadays. It's as if I'm interfering with their lives."

Margaret looked fondly at an old family photo on her dressing-table — she and Bob with their three children on a sandy beach.

"They'll be here," Bob announced with confidence, giving a last inspection of his brief-case before locking it, and glancing at his watch.

"I suppose you've planned a fantastic meal for them as usual."

He slipped on his jacket.

"All the old family favourites," Margaret replied. "You know me, the freezer's bursting with food. I keep forgetting that there's only the two of us to feed most of the time."

"And there's plenty of my good wine to wash it down . . . Now, darling, I'd better get going if I'm going to catch that plane."

He took his wife into his arms and kissed her tenderly.

"Goodbye, love," he whispered. "Have a happy birthday — but remember to miss me!" he said.

Together they walked to the car and Margaret returned his final wave as he drove away towards the airport.

NOW her birthday morning had arrived. Their double bed felt strangely wide without Bob beside her. But then the old familiar flutter of excitement for this special day surprised her and she hurried downstairs in her dressing-gown.

A pile of post lay on the hall mat. She scooped it up and settled down with her coffee to sort it out.

"Now, who's this from . . . ?"

Margaret examined the handwriting carefully before opening it. It was a game she had played for years, trying to guess the identity of the writer. Forty-nine and still playing games like a little girl!

But she didn't *feel* forty-nine, despite grey strands in her brown curls and laughter lines near her mouth that were etched too deeply.

"Susie . . ." She identified her daughter's large scrawl, green ink on purple paper. "Jamie . . ." Her elder son's neat handwriting was quite distinctive . . ." But nothing from young Craig . . . ah, yes, here it is!"

Briskly, she sorted through the letters again and stopped at a white envelope puzzled by the handwriting.

"Mother." She smiled, recognising the hand. "Dear Mother. She never forgets."

She looked more carefully at the writing and paused. Of course, it *was* from Mother, wasn't it? But mother didn't write like this!

This was written by an old lady with a shaky hand, and Mother wasn't . . . Mother *couldn't* be so old . . .

Margaret tore it open. The picture on the card could have been of distant Netherfield, Mother's village — a duck pond, tiny cottages, a profusion of wild flowers . . .

To my daughter Margaret on her birthday. God bless you, dear. Love, Mother.

Margaret gazed at the message. It was difficult to make it out. The arthritis in Mother's hands must be much worse than she admitted. Perhaps she should see a specialist.

Perhaps if Margaret insisted, she would agree to having "Meals-on-Wheels," allow visits from the local social services, admit to her deafness and wear a hearing aid . . . come and stay with them — even for a short visit.

War mums! They were a special breed. Independent, uncomplaining, proud. And Mum was a War *widow*.

On how many birthdays had she woken up alone in her solitary bed?

The telephone chirped in the hall breaking into her thoughts.

"Mum!" The voice was breathless. "It's me, Susie. Happy birthday, Mum! Can't speak for long — there's a queue a mile long outside the booth. Phone's out of order at the flat and I'm taking my portfolio to another designer and . . ."

"Will I see you tonight, dear?" Margaret asked her daughter.

"Hope so! It really depends on — gosh, I'm out of money —"

"But . . ."

"T'ra — I'll ring —"

Margaret replaced the receiver. That was typical of Susie — Susie the scatterbrain — sweet, secure Sue.

Margaret opened the fridge and reviewed the packed shelves.

"Enough to feed an army," she could hear her mother say. "If you don't eat your crusts your hair won't grow curly . . . eat up your custard like a good girl, just for Mummy . . ."

Memories of her childhood came flooding back.

Margaret slammed the fridge door shut and leant heavily against it.

WHERE had all the years gone? Those years of closeness with Mother — when Mother was youthful, agile, fiercelessly protective of her only child?

The things they had shared . . . hiding together beneath the stairs while the warning siren wailed sickeningly, jolly birthday parties with food hoarded from rations; the misery of Father's death; the excitement of school success; the joy of her marriage to Bob, and the miracle of the children's births.

They had shared so much for so long — and then, with her own family's pressures, somehow Mother was no longer a priority. Uncomplaining, undemanding, she had retreated into her quiet self.

And now, suddenly, before she realised, Mother was old!

Margaret stared again at the card her mother had sent, guilt and fear stirring in her like a dull ache.

I'll come to see you as soon as I can, she had written in her last letter — but that seemed ages ago! *I have so little free time at the moment . . .*

She *had* to write because Mother couldn't hear her clearly on the phone, but Mother rarely replied to her letters. It must be her hands . . . the pain?

"I'm perfectly all right on my own, ducky," Mother always insisted. "Don't you worry about me, my girl . . . you've got enough to think about!"

Spring's Rebirth

A GENTLER season gives the greening prize
When long-missed, moon-kissed, misty nights glow,
When half-forgotten faith gains grace to grow,
And spring's song comes strong, a soft breeze sighs.

Unmourned, old winter's ultimate demise
Means soft warm winds melt the snow
They blow the sun's cloud shroud away, to show
How fast remorseless time flies!

Those lank-flanked new lambs are glad they're not late.
Feathered twosomes are fashioning fine nests,
While the larks all sing, and ravens make their raucous cries;
And roaming rivers, foaming in flooded spate,
Are glimpsed in glinting hints from high hilltops' crests.
Spring is reborn as winter slowly dies.
— *Dan Pugh.*

Margaret hesitated for one moment more, then she tore open the rest of the post and arranged her cards unceremoniously along the kitchen window-sill. She dashed upstairs and dressed quickly. The unmade bed reminded her of her disorderly teenage years.

With a wicked grin she closed the bedroom door on its untidiness, hurried downstairs, and filled her shopping bag with an assortment of cooked dishes from the freezer.

She propped a scribbled note against the telephone. No-one could miss it — it was the traditional place for leaving messages for her family. She closed the front door behind her, banishing thoughts of what her children might think, and hurried towards the railway station.

★　　　★　　　★　　　★

The usually tedious journey to Netherfield seemed endless today. Perhaps she was wrong to come. Perhaps her unexpected arrival might frighten the frail old lady, excite her too greatly. Who could tell what the consequences might be?

"I do have some friends in the village," she remembered her mother telling her, although Margaret knew little of the old lady's daily routine. Yet she was always so interested in hearing news of her grandchildren . . .

"Netherfield — at last."

Margaret jumped off the train when it finally slowed to a halt, clutching her basket full of nourishing dishes for Mother.

The walk to the lane took her no time at all. The sun was still shining when she rushed up the stone pathway to Mother's front door.

She hesitated to open the door, suddenly afraid, although the key Mother had given her was in her hand.

She took a deep breath and rang the bell. The curtain twitched, she heard a shuffle inside.

The door jerked open.

"Yes? Can I help you?"

The smile froze on Margaret's face. Why was this unfamiliar woman in a tailored dark blue dress standing in Mother's hallway?

M ARGARET — I'm Margaret — her daughter!" She gasped. "What's happened? What's —"

"Oh, so *you* are Margaret! How strange! Come in, do."

Fearfully, Margaret crept along the dark hall towards the sunny kitchen from which there came a low mumble of voices.

Was this a nurse? Was Mother very sick? What was she about to discover? She reached the far room.

"Mother!" Margaret exclaimed.

There was her mother, fragile and pale, her white hair gently waved, a touch of pink lipstick on her lips, sitting at the table, surrounded by several equally stylish ladies of a similar age.

Before her was a pretty iced birthday cake and plates of dainty sandwiches.

Mother looked up in surprise.

"Why, Margaret, ducky! How lovely to see you! Is there anything wrong?"

Margaret stood awkwardly, feeling very much like a child at a grown-ups' party.

"No, Mother. Er — nothing's the matter."

She planted a kiss on her mother's papery cheek. "It's — it's my birthday. And . . . and I wanted to come home to you. To spend it with you — to say thank you," she finished lamely.

"Speak up, dear. My hearing, you know . . . You've come to visit! How nice!"

Mother held out her arms and Margaret knelt down beside her, hugging her close. Unexpected tears started in her eyes and flowed unchecked down her cheeks, as though time had never passed and she were a little girl.

"There, there, ducky . . . Tears? What are the tears for?" Mother rocked her gently in her arms, smoothing her hair.

"Of course it's your birthday!" she continued. "That's why I'm having a party for you with my friends — just like the old days. Remember? Only I didn't expect *you'd* be here with me — what with your family and everything . . ."

"But I was frightened — suddenly frightened . . ."

Mother sat back in her chair and looked intently at her daughter for a moment or two.

"I think I understand, Margaret," she said.

She paused and then, "We all have to get old, ducky. Even I'll have to get old, some time . . . but you mustn't worry, you mustn't worry about things you can't change, eh? And now, dry your eyes and let's introduce you to my friends and then we'll have some birthday cake."

Margaret smiled gratefully as the ladies wished her happy birthday. Then, above the chatter she heard the sound of the telephone ringing in the hall.

"I'll answer it," she told her mother's friend in the dark blue dress. "I think it's for me," she added, walking back into the hall and picking up the receiver.

HELLO! Is that you, Mum? It's Susie here. I say, Mum, what a laugh you dumping us with the microwave and the freezer — and Dad's best wine and zooming off —"

"Sorry, darling! I hope you don't mind. I just wanted — " Her voice choked.

"You just wanted to go and spend your special day with Gran! I know, Mum. How is she? Give her our love. We're having a terrific time here. It's just like the old days when we were here on our own! The others want to speak to you . . ."

Margaret listened while her three children shouted their good wishes in turn.

"Are you going to stay there for a bit, Mum, with Gran?" Susie was back in charge.

"Why don't you, while Daddy's away? You must have so much to talk about, about when you were little, and everything . . . It must be lovely having her all to yourself again."

Margaret paused, surprised at the depth of her young daughter's understanding.

"W-ell . . . well yes, for a couple of days. And I shall be coming here more often . . ."

"Don't worry about a thing here. We'll leave it all tidy — lock everything up when we leave. I've got this amazing interview tomorrow with a new designer. It's so hectic for all of us . . . Anyway, give our love to Gran. Have a wonderful time. And happy birthday!"

Margaret smiled to herself as she made her way back to sample the birthday cake.

How well her children understood. Traditional birthday celebrations were very nice, but . . .

Why couldn't they be "Thank you, Mother" days instead, while it was still possible? For surely, without our mothers none of us would be here! □

they were first...

ON top of the world — that's how Edmund Hillary and Sherpa Tenzing must have felt on the morning of the May 29, 1953. For that's when the New Zealander and his Nepalese companion stood on the summit of Mount Everest — a feat no-one had achieved before them.

Hillary was knighted that same year, and five years later chalked up another "first," when as a member of the New Zealand Antarctic Expedition, he was the first man since Amundsen to reach the South Pole.

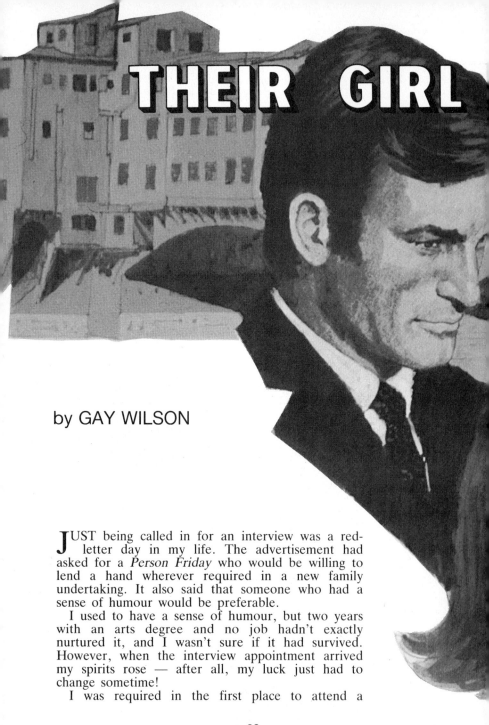

THEIR GIRL

by GAY WILSON

JUST being called in for an interview was a red-letter day in my life. The advertisement had asked for a *Person Friday* who would be willing to lend a hand wherever required in a new family undertaking. It also said that someone who had a sense of humour would be preferable.

I used to have a sense of humour, but two years with an arts degree and no job hadn't exactly nurtured it, and I wasn't sure if it had survived. However, when the interview appointment arrived my spirits rose — after all, my luck just had to change sometime!

I was required in the first place to attend a

FRIDAY !

preliminary rendezvous in Oxford, and found the building easily enough. It was while I was peering at brass plates on doors down a seemingly-endless corridor that I bumped into the brown man!

"Sorry!" we both exclaimed simultaneously, he with a much more friendly expression than me.

"You look sort of lost," he said. "Are you?"

He had a nice ordinary face with brown hair and eyes, and wore a brown jacket over a check shirt. I knew why I had instinctively labelled him the "brown man," for he had a sort of outdoorish glow about him which was tremendously attractive.

"I'm looking for these people," I said, showing him my letter. "I've got an interview for a job."

"Ah!" His face cleared. "You'll be one of the Friday Persons."

"I hope so," I said.

"I do, too!" His eyes twinkled.

"Follow me," he said, turning on his heel, and I did — clip-clopping a bit in my sister's expensive shoes which were half a size too big for me but gloriously elegant and had actually been offered for my big day.

The interview-room was already occupied. There were five female and four male would-be Friday Persons and I appeared to be the last.

"D'you know what all this is about?" the brown man whispered, as he found me a chair.

I shook my head. "I only know that it's some sort of family enterprise."

"It's Aubrey Overton's," he said with a grin. "He's opening up his ancestral home — not because he wants to, but because he *has* to. It's either that or sell up, so naturally he requires staff to run it."

"It sounds really interesting," I said, and my heart beat quickly. "Are you an applicant, too?"

"I'm a humble PRO man," he replied briefly. "Just about to give this little company here the once-over. I wish they didn't look so scared."

"I think they're anxious more than scared," I said. "Being unemployed makes you like that. You lose confidence in yourself."

"Surely not you?" He gave me a long look, eyebrows raised.

"Worst of all me!" I said.

He leaned forward. "Let me give you a tip. When you get inside the holy of holies, don't let it show. Old Aubrey's a bit of a bully and he hates mouse types. Say what you want to say and don't be intimidated. He loves girls with a bit of spirit."

He gave me a reassuring smile as he prepared to move off.

"Remember what I've told you, and the best of luck."

THE selection committee was rather elderly and slightly pompous. Also frightening. I realised at once that the one with the bristling moustache was Aubrey Overton and he seemed to be firing most of the questions.

"You are Miss Fiona Leigh?" he said, peering at his pile of papers, and then peering across the desk at me above his bi-focals.

"What d'you think you can do to help run a small estate for the benefit of the public? There'll be entertainment for children, teas, an adventure playground. Greenhouses of rare tropical plants, a historic mansion full of valuable pictures, tapestries, armour and the like. A bookshop, of course, and souvenirs . . ."

"I can bake and serve in the tearoom," I said as confidently as I could manage. "I could supervise children in the adventure playground so that their parents could look over the manor in a relaxed atmosphere. There again, I could show people over the house and learn how to present its treasures."

I was warming to the task.

"I could help in the greenhouses, or sit at a desk handing out leaflets or whatever," I went on. "I could serve in the bookshop, or keep accounts. I could even render First Aid if this should ever become necessary!"

I stopped for breath, appalled at myself and blaming the brown man for my arrogance.

"Umm . . ." remarked Aubrey Overton. "And where and how did you manage to learn so much?"

I felt my face go unbecomingly red.

"Mostly at home," I said in my normal humble voice. "Partly at college, at the Red Cross, and during one or two voluntary jobs I've done since leaving school."

"Umm . . ." he said again, and the elderly gentleman on his right muttered something which I didn't quite catch but which sounded like "living in."

"I'm prepared to live in, too," I said before I could check myself, "and I've just passed my driving test."

"Thank you, Miss Leigh," said old Aubrey solemnly. "Thank you very much indeed. We'll let you know."

My heart sank at the too-familiar words. I'd been cherishing the hope that I'd be told right away. But I stood up, managed a bright smile, said good afternoon and walked out with my back erect.

I hadn't expected to see the brown man again, but as I passed through the waiting-room, he was busy scribbling with a notepad on his knee. He looked up as I approached and I had the feeling he'd been waiting for me.

"How did it go?" he asked.

"I'm not sure. I did what you suggested, but I have a terrible feeling they'll think I'm boastful and write me off."

"What did they say?"

"The usual, they'd let me know."

"Cheer up," he said. "I think they'll realise how well you would fit into the scheme. You are just the girl they are looking for."

I tried to smile, but all the hopeful euphoria of the morning had evaporated. I felt dehydrated as though I'd spilled everything out of myself and now there was nothing left.

"What you need," the brown man was saying, "is a bite of lunch.

What about popping over to the Wellow Arms across the road, or perhaps we could drive as far as Banbury? There's a little eating-house I know there. Afterwards I could show you Aubrey's manor."

"I'd like that," I said. "Even if I never see it again, I'd like to see it today."

We feasted on rainbow trout stuffed with mushrooms, followed by banana splits and coffee and then we drove out to the manor.

IT was enchanting. Not too large, with creeper-covered walls and tall Elizabethan chimneys.

It stood in about forty acres of beautiful garden which was divided into walks — Cherry Tree Walk, Rhododendron Walk, Azalea Walk, etc., and there was a genuine camomile lawn surrounded with lavender in front of a gazebo. It was in mint condition although obviously of a later design than the manor itself.

"Teas!" I exclaimed excitedly. "Teas could be served from here. Old-fashioned simnel cakes and Bath buns! The waitresses could wear mob caps and kirtles and buckled shoes. Think of the atmosphere."

He was looking at me in a way which made me blush.

"You're right," he said, and stopped suddenly. "Atmosphere, that's what we need. If the place has to be commercialised let's do it thoroughly."

"A Tudor manor house must be run by wenches and yokels," I said, grinning happily.

He grinned back. "Any more ideas?"

"A croquet lawn . . . and archery. You know the bowman of Olde England sort of thing, Good Queen Bess and all that."

He laughed out loud. "You're an inspiration, young lady, and I don't even know your name."

"I don't know yours either," I retorted.

"Mine," he said, sweeping me a bow, "Robin Goodfellow — how could it be otherwise?"

He was laughing, but there was wariness in his brown eyes.

I entered into his mood. "And I'm Nell Gwynn," I said. "I've left my orange basket in the car."

We had a most stimulating afternoon exploring Aubrey's manor and I knew I would always remember the brown man although I doubted I would ever see him again. Later he drove me back to Oxford and saw me on to my train.

"Goodbye, Mistress Nell. We must keep in contact — by runner, of course. Telephones aren't yet invented. I might even have some news for you — or you might have some for me."

I met his enigmatic gaze.

"Thank you for a lovely day," I said, and then I had to turn away for a lump had arisen in my throat which was quite unaccountable.

He raised my hand halfway to his lips with mock gravity. My brown man certainly had a sense of humour, and he had something else as well which I knew I would remember always.

I knew, too, that if he wanted to see me again, he would find a way of arranging it. With this thought I comforted myself as the train moved out of the station.

★　　★　　★　　★

The letter came one week later. It was courteous and strictly to the point. It thanked me for attending the interview in Oxford. The vacancy had now been filled but they wished me well.

Every scrap of brightness went out of the morning sunshine and I realised how much I'd been counting on a lucky break.

To keep up my spirits I washed my hair, using a new exciting colour rinse, then I sat down at the table and scanned the *Situations Vacant* columns in the papers.

I had a vague idea of applying for a domestic situation, possibly abroad. After all, caring for children could be, if not soul satisfactory, at least worthwhile.

And then as I sat there half-reading, half-brooding, the phone rang. It was him!

"Is that Mistress Nell?"

"Hello," I said dejectedly.

"Thank you for ringing, but the news is bad. I didn't get the job."

"I know," he said calmly. "I arranged it!"

"You what?"

On Hilltop High

THE hilltop view is fine and grand —
　　the whole world lies below,
And from a cottage, far away, a wisp
　　of smoke may show.
There's not a sound except the wind,
　　that whispers in your ear,
And all around, high over all, the sky
　　so blue and clear.

Escape is grand when you can find a
　　lonely hilltop crest,
Then you feel, within your soul, the
　　peace that is the best.
And though you must go back to town,
　　where life is never still,
You'll take with you the joy you found,
　　upon the quiet hill.
　　　　　　　　　— *Georgina Hall.*

"I arranged that you didn't get the job. Not that one, anyway. I've got a much better proposition for the likes of you, but I had to get approval first. You see, I'm only the dogsbody in the set-up."

"I wish I knew what you are talking about," I said.

"I can understand that. Now before you start throwing oranges at me, hear me out. Do you know The Ring o' Bells on the London road near your place?"

"What's that got to do with it?"

"I want to meet you there. Now. Can you make it?"

"I suppose I could."

"Then get going, girl. I'm already there tearing out my hair."

"Leave a tuft," I said, regaining a flash of my sense of humour. "I can't stand baldies."

"OK, my love. Be seeing you."

I put the phone down in a daze. He was waiting for me at The Ring o' Bells, and he had called me "my love"!

HE looked different when we met. He was still wearing brown, but this time an immaculate suit with a silk tie and hand-kerchief to match.

I felt dreadfully shy until he took my hands into his own and said with that devastating smile:

"You'll have to forgive me, Fiona —"

"You do know my name," I interrupted.

"I know more than that," he said, "and I suppose it's only fair you should know mine."

He was serious now! Anxious, in fact.

"I'm Lindsay Overton. Old Aubrey is my uncle, and the manor is my eventual inheritance. The scheme to keep it solvent is my dream child."

I was so shattered by this revelation I couldn't speak for a moment. Then I said coldly, "I don't know what all this has to do with me."

"Don't be angry," he pleaded. "I know I'm handling this badly. I'm not a good organiser and I'm impulsive, but I saw it all when we were walking together in the manor grounds.

"You made it all come alive . . . call it the woman's touch, I don't know. You supplied the missing inspiration."

"I still don't get it. If I'm so good, why didn't I get the job?"

"Because you're too good and it wasn't the right job. I'm offering you an alternative. I want you as a Personal Assistant not a Girl Friday. I had the devil of a job to convince my uncle of this.

"He wanted you for himself. He took to you right away. I knew he would if you didn't let him bully you."

He stopped suddenly and spread out his hands. "I suppose I've put my foot in it as usual and you won't speak to me any more."

"You must be j-joking," I sobbed, as I blew my nose and pinched myself to prove I wasn't dreaming.

"I've never been more serious in my life. We've been looking for someone like you long before we advertised for the Friday Persons."

His hands were on my shoulders now, warm and protective. "I shouldn't have blurted it out like that. My uncle says I lack finesse, and he's dead right."

I didn't realise how close we were until the roughness of his jacket brushed my cheek.

"Go home," he said gently, "and think it over. I'll be in touch in a day or so."

"By runner?" I managed to whisper.

"Not . . . likely!" he exploded, and although he didn't kiss me, I knew he wanted to. □

The Best Of All . . .

THERE'S a lot to be said for a day
   at sea,
Watching the young folk romping with
  glee.
Or maybe you fancy a hike up a hill,
With heather that's blooming so quiet
  and still.
If money is short, there's always
  the park,
With a girl on your arm, it can be quite
  a lark.
But the best place of all, as everyone
  knows,
Is a home of your own where happiness
  grows.
You're sure of a welcome, warm and
  sweet,
With so many loving faces to greet!

              — *Miriam Eker.*

D ONNA McBRIDE
hurried along Hilltop
Crescent to her sister's
house at No. 9. It was her
lunch break from the building
society office where she
worked — and the most
convenient time to talk to
Alison.

"Will soup and a sandwich
do?" Alison had asked over
the telephone. "I have to go
out at two. I'm working
part-time at the hospital."

"That will be fine," Donna
told her. "But make it a
doorstep. You know what my
appetite is like!"

"What do you want to see
me about that's so urgent?"
Alison asked as both girls sat
down at the kitchen table.

"This soup's good. Yes,
well . . . I've got a great idea
for Mum and Dad's silver
wedding gift. Do you
remember how often Mum has
regretted that she and Dad ran
completely out of money after
they got married, and never
managed to pick up the
photographs of the wedding?"

"Yes, I know. I've heard
her talking about it often
enough."

Donna leaned across the
table as she bit into her
sandwich.

"Suppose we get a portrait
photograph of them for their
silver wedding, and put it in a
silver frame," she said
between mouthfuls. "We're all
going out to Chez Louis for
the celebration, and we can
present it to them there."

Alison stared at her sister

thoughtfully, then she nodded.

"That's not a bad idea, Donna. We'd better not go to Meiklejohn's, though. I think Mum still gets embarrassed every time she passes the door."

"Why not go there? They'll never rememeber what happened twenty-five years ago, and they're the only good photographers in town."

▶over

by JEAN MELVILLE

After All Those Years

"I suppose you're right," Alison conceded. "I tell you what, I could meet you on Saturday in town. Colin is working in Glasgow this weekend, and we could go to Meiklejohn's together."

"You're on," Donna said with a grin. "We'll tackle Meiklejohn's together." Her eyes sobered for a moment. "It won't be a surprise, though, since we would have to let Mum and Dad in on the secret. After all, they'll have to sit for the photograph."

"We'd better find out about costs first," Alison said. "Now that Colin and I are married, I'm not that much better off than Mum and Dad were in those early days."

"At least you *are* married," Donna said. "Derek and I are still saving up."

★　　　★　　　★　　　★

Meiklejohn's the photographers, weren't quite in their usual orderly state when both girls called there the following Saturday afternoon. They had to walk over one of two planks and under a ladder before a flustered young man hurried out from the back to talk to them.

"We're a bit disorganised," he apologised, "but if you'll come through to the studio here, it's better. I haven't long taken over the business since Mrs Meiklejohn retired, and I'm afraid the premises need quite a bit of modernisation."

"Yes, I can see what you mean." Donna nodded, eyeing the lovely old wood being ripped away from the walls. Privately she thought it a pity.

"The business goes back to old Arnold Meiklejohn's time, Alex Meiklejohn's father, but Alex died two years ago and Mrs Meiklejohn has carried on since then. I was her assistant, but I've taken over now.

"Now, what can I do for you two ladies? Do you want to be photographed together, or separately?"

"Neither," Donna told him. "We want an estimate for a portrait of our parents, to be put in a silver frame. It's for their silver wedding anniversary."

"What size of photograph do you have in mind? We can do the proofs, of course, and you can choose from them, but if you want an estimate . . . well . . ."

The new photographer began to produce a selection of photographs, together with a price list.

"We don't do silver frames, of course. You'd have to get that at the jeweller's, and it might cost you a bit. We could do a photograph to fit whichever size you choose."

DONNA and Alison were looking at the prices with a hint of dismay. Alison had already priced the silver frames and she bit her lip. The gift idea was wonderful, but could she and Donna afford it?

"Maybe we'll have to think about it a little more," Donna said in a low voice. Then she laughed and shook her head.

"Twenty-five years ago, our parents were married and had their photograph taken here. A whole album, in fact. Unfortunately . . . they couldn't afford to pick it up. My mother was very disappointed and very embarrassed about it. She's never really got over it.

"We thought we would put it all right with a new photograph, but with the price of the frame, it's going to be quite expensive."

"More than it would have been twenty-five years ago," the young man admitted. "I'm afraid costs have gone up a little since then! That would be in Alex Meiklejohn's time."

He stared at them for a moment.

"You know, when Mrs Meiklejohn moved out, she took away boxes and boxes of old files, negatives and such-like from the attic. There's just a chance that she might still have that old album. You never know . . ."

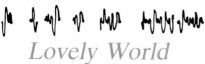

Lovely World

ISN'T it a lovely world,
  With birds and flowers and trees,
The scent of roses, new-mown hay,
And wonders such as these.

  Isn't it a lovely world —
    Behold a summer's sky,
  Gentle breezes, sunlit days,
    The rainbow's arc on high.

      There's so much wonder all around
        As nature's joys unfurled,
      Look with your eyes — say with
        your heart —
      It is a lovely world.
          — *Sylvia Mountain.*

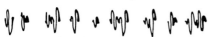

"You're kidding!" Donna exclaimed.

"Yes, I know it's stretching things a little but nothing ventured . . . Anyway, you could always ask her. I'll write down the address for you."

"I very much doubt if she would still have the album," Alison put in. She was picking up one of the samples. "Perhaps we could have one of these smaller ones, and a simpler frame."

Donna looked at the sample her sister indicated. She turned to her sister, her eyes beginning to sparkle. "We'll bear that in mind, but wouldn't it be great if we could find the *original* photographs of Mum and Dad? It would be such a surprise for them. I would pay for that album, whatever it cost. Wouldn't you?"

"Definitely," Alison agreed, fired by her enthusiasm.

"You've been very kind," Donna said to the young photographer. "Maybe we'll be back to talk to you again."

"Any time," he assured them. "Good luck. She's a nice lady or I wouldn't send you to her."

FLORA MEIKLEJOHN had not had a good morning. She hadn't been able to sleep the previous night and had lain for hours listening to the radio before eventually falling asleep.

Now she felt heavy-eyed and cross with herself. She really would have to do something about her house. It was far too big for her on her own. It had belonged to Alex's parents and grandparents before them.

Alex had been ten years older than herself, and when he died two years ago, he had still been in the saddle at seventy.

Mrs Meiklejohn had kept on the business, with the help of Alan Muir, until just a few months ago. Then she had worked out a scheme for Alan to buy the business from her.

She had felt so heartsick when she no longer had Alex at her elbow. They had done everything together and she had loved the work so much.

But on a morning such as this, Flora Meiklejohn felt depressed, and wondered why she had given up so easily. She was only sixty-two. She could have carried on for another three years at least. And Alan was now busy pulling the place apart.

He didn't see the soft mellow patina of the old wood which gave the premises an air of tradition. He would only want modern plastic and chipboard.

She had decided to go shopping in the afternoon when the bell rang, and she opened the door to two young ladies. It was easy to see they were sisters and both of them wore a slightly apprehensive look in their brown eyes.

"I'm Donna McBride, and this is my sister, Mrs Alison Ramsay," the younger one said, stepping forward. "We don't want to be a nuisance to you, Mrs Meiklejohn, but we wondered if we could have a word with you? Mr . . . er, the young man at the photographer's gave us your address."

"Please come in," Mrs Meiklejohn invited.

Between them, speaking rather hesitantly, the two girls began to tell Flora Meiklejohn their story.

"We might be asking for completely the impossible, and I suppose you've got a right to be annoyed," Donna ended finally, "but do you think you might *still* have that album?"

"I really couldn't say," Mrs Meiklejohn told them. "However, I will have a note of it in my records." She stood up. "There's a chance the photographs may still exist. The only way to find out is if we all go upstairs and check the ledgers."

How quiet and peaceful the old house seemed, Donna thought, as she climbed the red-carpeted stairs. The wood panelling was similar to that which was being destroyed at the shop, and she liked the solid staircase and the polished wood doors with brass handles.

Mrs Meiklejohn led the way to the attic, then swept her arm around as they gazed at the many, many boxes of old photographs and negatives which were piled up on the floor.

"Now, let me see . . ." She pulled a ledger from the drawer of the desk. "You have the date, of course?"

Donna was staring at the boxes as Alison told the older woman the date of her parents' wedding.

The older woman ran a finger through the ledger.

"Ah, yes," she said, "here it is!"

She looked up and closed the book.

"Now let me see . . . if it is here it'll be somewhere in that pile over there." She nodded to what seemed to Donna to be a huge heap in the faraway corner.

"It's probably in no fit condition to be given to anyone, but the negatives should be there. I wonder . . ."

Donna felt her pulse quicken. "Would it be all right if Alison and I helped you look. Tomorrow, perhaps? Will Colin still be away tomorrow, Alison?"

"Until about eight o'clock," Alison said.

Mrs Meiklejohn looked at the two hopeful faces.

"Let's put the kettle on," she said. "Perhaps we could work together to see if your album's there, though it won't be an easy task."

"Nothing is easy until you start," Donna told her.

FOR Flora Meiklejohn, the next day and the following few evenings were the happiest — and the saddest — she had spent for some time. It was as though she were saying goodbye to Alex as she went through the boxes and remembered the work they had done together over so many years.

Alison had been forced to give up her part of the search after Colin returned home, but Donna continued to arrive each evening, and Flora Meiklejohn began to look forward to her company.

"I love your beautiful old house," Donna said as they climbed the stairs together. "Some day Derek and I will be well off and perhaps we can buy a house like this."

She laughed lightly. "We can't even get a flat at the moment, but we do love to dream."

"You're engaged to be married?"

"Yes, since last Christmas. Derek is away on a course. He's training to be an estate agent. That's why I know we'll have a nice house one day."

"I'm sure you will." Mrs Meiklejohn smiled.

Two nights later the older woman found the album in a cardboard box, and Donna's eyes filled with tears when they eventually carried it downstairs. There was something very poignant about looking at her parents on their wedding day, also their grandparents, two of whom were now dead.

"It's in no fit state to present to your parents like this," Mrs Meiklejohn said, "but here are the negatives. We'll get Alan to do a fresh copy."

"Oh, goodness . . . how much will that cost?" Donna asked.

"Less than he quoted for the new photograph," Mrs Meiklejohn said drily. "I'll see him about it, dear."

"But would it be ready for our evening out at Chez Louis?" Donna asked eagerly. "What a surprise it would be! It should be a marvellous evening, Mrs Meiklejohn. Derek is coming home specially, also my sister and her husband, Granny McBride, and Grandpa Arnott.

"Look . . . why don't you come, too? Everyone would love you to be there, and when my parents know the full story you'll be the guest of honour."

Mrs Meiklejohn was laughing.

"No, my dear, it's very kind of you, but it's a *family* occasion and very special. But bring your Derek to meet me the following day . . . Sunday, isn't it? Come for tea and you can both tell me all about it. Will that do?"

"I'll bring you a piece of cake," Donna promised.

Mrs Meiklejohn watched from the window as Donna went down the garden path. Then her eyes roamed round the room, before she went out into the hall and assessed the stairs. Yes, the house could be turned into two flats, she thought. And she was sure the girl and her young man were a nice couple.

It was certainly an idea to be turned over in her mind most carefully, but even the thought of it was bringing new life into her step as she walked through to the kitchen to prepare her tea.

THE table at Chez Louis was beautifully set for a silver wedding party, and as Ruth McBride looked round her family, her heart overflowed. She wiped away a tear, remembering how she and Dave had not always found life easy, but how rewarding it was to be here now.

Her two lovely daughters were grown up, with two fine young men by their side, loving them as surely as Dave had loved her. She felt sad that her father and Dave's mother could not be with them, but their memory was still dear to their hearts.

On the table she could see a collection of gifts for them to open, but the excitement was almost electric as they opened their present from the girls. Then both Ruth and Dave McBride stared speechlessly at the photographs which had been taken on their wedding day, twenty-five years before.

"I . . . I don't believe it," Ruth said at last.

"It . . . it's a miracle," Dave managed. "Where did you get them, Alison . . . Donna?"

"Yes, *how* did you girls manage this?" Ruth asked, hardly seeing the photographs for the tears which were dancing in her eyes.

"It's a long story," Alison said, laughing.

"We knew you would want the photographs if we could get them," Donna was saying.

"It really is like a miracle," Dave was saying again, then he looked closely at the wedding photographs, and turned to his wife. "Ruth, darling, you haven't changed a bit!"

"Oh, Dave." She gasped.

Tears turned to laughter and Ruth's face was radiant as she looked at her family.

"I've never been so happy," she said, as the album was passed round for all to see. "Never — except, perhaps, on my wedding day."

She looked into her husband's smiling face.

★   ★   ★   ★

"And after that," Donna told Mrs Meiklejohn excitedly, "the waiter brought champagne and we all had a piece of cake. Didn't we, Derek?"

Derek nodded and grinned at Mrs Meiklejohn. They had taken an immediate liking to one another.

"Just like this piece," he said, offering it to her.

"Maybe I'll have a wedding cake of my own one of these days," Donna said, dreaming again.

Mrs Meiklejohn smiled at Derek.

"Maybe you will," she agreed.

And for the moment, she felt, that was enough. □

they were first...

IN May 1930, less than a year after gaining her pilot's licence, Amy Johnson set off from Croydon, outside London. Her aim was to become the first woman to fly solo from Europe to Australia — a journey of some 12,000 miles.

Her plane was a tiny Gypsy Moth — and the trip was beset by difficulties. She was forced down three times, and it was some nineteen days after leaving that she finally arrived at Darwin — to a rapturous reception.

THE BEST GIFT OF ALL

AS the excited screams of the children next door echoed over the garden wall, Ed Warren frowned. For the umpteenth time he railed silently at the now departed Chisholmes for selling their house to a family with young children.

Now, he'd never have a moment's peace — and Ed was used to a quiet life.

' He finished cutting away some dead flower stalks and winced as yet another squeal sounded from next door. He was used to much more subdued sounds. Summer sounds like the buzz of bees in his garden, the drone of a lawn mower and the muffled silence of snow-filled winters with perhaps the distant wailing of a storm heard from the cosy shelter of his home.

The wails and screams of young children were a different matter altogether. He'd never get used to them. Not at his time of life.

He supposed much of his attitude stemmed from the fact that his late wife, Muriel, and himself had never been blessed with children of

46

their own. The family they expected to have had never materialised
and by the time they had got around to contemplating adoption it
was too late.

Muriel had always comforted him with the words that they had
each other and that was enough, but Ed had caught the occasional
sadness and wistfulness of her expression when she saw a young
child. Now she was gone and Ed had no-one. A few cousins scattered
over the country and the odd bowling companion.

At seventy-four Ed found few of his contemporaries left to offer
him companionship in his old age. He had been half hoping an

elderly couple would move next door. He'd seen a few viewing the house.

Then these Elliots have moved in with their three fair-haired, exuberant children — two little girls and a boy who looked the youngest of the three.

Ed dumped the debris into his wheelbarrow and straightened his back gingerly. There was nothing to be done about this latest situation. Short of moving himself, what could he do?

A missile came sailing over the garden wall and struck his shoulder.

"What in the name . . . ?" He looked around as a brightly-coloured ball bounced on the path behind him then rolled at his feet.

He picked it up and glanced towards the dividing wall with a frown of irritation — just as a small, tow-coloured head bobbed into view.

"Could I have my ball back, please, mister?"

Ed gazed at the small face silently for a moment, then with a grunt chucked the ball back over the wall.

"Thanks."

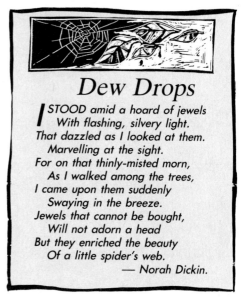

Dew Drops

I STOOD amid a hoard of jewels
   With flashing, silvery light.
That dazzled as I looked at them.
   Marvelling at the sight.
For on that thinly-misted morn,
   As I walked among the trees,
I came upon them suddenly
   Swaying in the breeze.
Jewels that cannot be bought,
   Will not adorn a head
But they enriched the beauty
   Of a little spider's web.
           — Norah Dickin.

The boy smiled at Ed but instead of disappearing to fetch his ball he stayed put, eyes sweeping Ed's garden with interest, before settling with great friendliness on Ed himself.

"You have a very nice garden," he said.

"Hmm," Ed muttered, wishing the child would just go.

The thought of being obliged to make small talk with children annoyed him, causing him to raise his voice slightly. "And I want it to stay that way. Perhaps in future you'll be more careful with that ball of yours."

He turned away and resumed his task of clearing up.

There was a short pause in which Ed breathed a sigh of relief thinking the child had gone. Then, "OK," the voice said brightly, not in the least abashed.

"My name's Chris Elliot. What's yours?"

Ed didn't attempt to suppress his grunt of annoyance. He considered ignoring the boy but he appeared to be one of those impossibly persistent children who kept at you with the tenacity of a gnat.

"Mr Warren," he muttered.

To his immediate relief a woman's voice called out just then.

"Chris! Lunch is ready. Where are you?"

The boy grinned. "That's my mum. Coming, Mum . . . What's your first name?"

Ed just stopped himself from saying that it was none of the boy's business. Perhaps it would be best to tell him and then maybe he would go.

"Ed," he muttered.

"I'll see you again, Ed. Got to get my lunch now."

"Don't hurry back," Ed grunted, as the small head bobbed out of sight.

WHY are you still working in your garden? It's nearly Christmas." Ed looked up to see Chris peering over the wall. He had resigned himself to the fact that most days he'd have the small boy's presence at the wall watching him working, asking him innumerable questions.

"There's work in a garden most times." He smiled. "Except maybe when it's snowing."

The small face lit up. "I love the snow. Do you think it'll snow for Santa coming? It rained last year."

"Perhaps it will. It's cold enough."

"Those leaves are pretty. What a pity they had to fall off the trees."

Ed toppled the barrowful of leaves into his compost heap.

"They've got to make room for the new leaves that'll be there next year," he explained. "Don't you go to school?"

"Of course, silly!" Chris said scornfully. "But I get out at three o'clock. It's almost four."

"It'll soon be dark," Ed grunted. "Isn't it time you went indoors? You'll catch cold."

There was a brief pause.

"What you said about the leaves . . ." The boy's voice was lower, hesitant. "That goes for people, too, doesn't it? When Papa died my mum said people died to make room for new people."

Ed gazed at the child through the gathering dusk. His eyes were downcast and his finger scratched repeatedly at the top of the brick wall.

"I didn't care about the new people," Chris murmured. "I only wanted Papa. He was *my* people. He was my best friend."

As Ed watched he saw the boy's lip tremble, heard the catch in his voice. He didn't know quite what to say.

"We all have to lose people we love," he said shortly.

Without another word Chris disappeared from the wall leaving Ed to gaze at the blank space where he'd been, his gaze quizzical.

★　　　★　　　★　　　★

The biting frosts came followed by the snow. Ed had to busy himself pottering about the house as the garden was out of bounds.

D

He felt oddly weary and kept dozing off in front of the TV set.

During these short, dark days he missed Muriel more than ever. Selfishly he wished he had been taken first, and then was sorry for the thought. Muriel had always been so dependent on him.

As a girl she had been so quiet and shy and as a woman she'd scarcely raised her voice, always looking to him for support. Not that she'd been dull. Muriel had never been dull with that constantly-smiling face and warm manner. Everyone had loved her.

Ed flicked a tear away with a gnarled thumb, annoyed with himself. His rheumatism had been troubling him lately and it was making him maudlin. He wished the weather would clear a bit so that he could get out into the garden. There were always bits and pieces to do there.

The thought of Chris intruded but he dismissed it as suddenly. It was the garden he missed, he told himself, not the incessant chatter of that child. But inside he knew differently . . .

THE thaw arrived, and with it, to Ed's disgust, his first burst pipe in years. When he awoke on the Monday morning his kitchen was flooded and he had to send for the plumber.

To calm his unsettled nerves Ed decided to potter around the garden for an hour. After half an hour he decided it had been an unwise decision. His back had never got over the last bout of rheumatism and ached through leaning over to mend the wooden edging that divided his vegetable garden from the rest. And there was no sign of the boy, which somehow made him even more tetchy.

"Hello, Ed!"

Ed looked up to see the blonde head, red capped for the weather, poised above the wall.

"Hello," he said, trying to disguise his pleasure.

"Mum says it's only about two weeks till Christmas and the snow's gone. What are you doing?"

Ed straightened gingerly, grimacing. "Mending the edging."

"I've asked Santa to bring me a red wooden engine for Christmas. Just like the one Papa had when he was a boy."

"Oh?" Ed grunted, wondering whether he should be inside and

▶p52

BUILT in 1895, Crathie Church is immediately recognisable as the place of worship for the Royal Family when they are in residence at nearby Balmoral Castle. Then, it seems, thousands make for this hamlet and pack the normally quiet roads around the church, hoping for a glimpse of the Queen. It was Queen Victoria who first came to Crathie, and inside the small church are memorials to various members of the Royal Family. In the graveyard is a monument Queen Victoria erected to John Brown, her faithful attendant. His house can be seen across the Dee from the kirkyard.

CRATHIE CHURCH, Aberdeenshire : J CAMPBELL KERR

take a couple of those pain killers the doctor had given him. Maybe while he was at it he should tackle the mess the plumber had left.

"Yes. Daddy said maybe Santa would bring me an electric train set instead. But I'd rather have a red engine like Papa's."

He eyed Ed with sudden concern. "What's wrong? Do you have a pain?"

On Ed's nod he continued, "Papa was always having pains, too. Why don't you see a doctor? I was ill and Mum called the doctor in . . ."

Ed winced again as another spasm of pain shot through his back.

"You're not going to die, are you?" the boy asked anxiously.

Ed's short temper flared.

"No!" he shouted. "I'm not going to die, you silly little boy. Now why don't you go play with your sisters!"

As he said the words the small boy's face turned pale, stricken. Even as Ed regretted them and moved forward, hand extended, the boy disappeared from view. Ed, furious with himself, cried after him.

"Chris! I'm sorry. I didn't mean . . . Oh blast!"

He hadn't meant to shout at the boy. It was the accumulation of things: the burst pipe, his rheumatic pain, his loneliness.

There. At last he had admitted it, but he didn't feel the better for it. At last he recognised the fact that Chris had done a lot to assuage that loneliness.

With the wintry weather he had missed the small boy's company and his incessant chatter. Now he had hurt him and he wondered what to do about it.

Ed was very busy over the next few days. He hovered constantly about the garden, too, hoping to see Chris, to apologise to his small friend but the boy didn't appear.

THROUGH working into the small hours Ed managed to finish his task by Christmas Eve and at nine o'clock that evening he approached the house next door — a clumsily-wrapped bundle in his arms.

He hesitated rather apprehensively on the front doorstep as the doorbell rang out, thinking about his churlish behaviour those days before.

Mrs Elliot opened the door, her fair skin flushed, her face smiling.

"Oh, hello. It's Mr Warren from next door, isn't it? Chris is always talking about you. I'm afraid he hasn't been well lately . . .

"Oh, nothing to worry about, really," she added as concern filled Ed's face. "He was just talking about you the other day, actually. Please come in. It's much too cold to stand on the doorstep."

Ed stepped inside, feeling embarrassed and rather foolish now as he clutched the awkward parcel in his arms.

"I won't keep you," he muttered. "I just popped in with this. It's for Chris. I, er . . . made it myself."

"Why, thank you. How kind." Mrs Elliot smiled. "Chris *will* be pleased."

"Well . . . don't let me keep you," Ed said, at a loss what to do now he'd handed over the gift. "I can tell you're busy."

"Nonsense. I've finished my baking now." Mrs Elliot went on to explain that Chris had a rather weak chest which gave him quite a bit of bother, which was the main reason they had moved nearer the country.

She looked down at the parcel and the tag with the hastily-scrawled words: *To Chris. Merry Christmas from your friend, Ed.*

"Chris will be pleased. He says you're his best friend." She smiled sadly. "He used to call my father that. He died, you know, a year ago. Chris missed him terribly when he died."

"Yes," Ed said. "He told me. To be quite honest, Mrs Elliot . . ." Ed fidgeted with his cap. "I was a bit short with him a few days ago. I've no excuse except that my rheumatism was bothering me, what with the burst pipe . . . but it's been worrying me."

Chris's mother smiled sympathetically.

"I know about that. But I think I managed to explain to him all right. Wait a moment. He made you something today. I meant to put it through your letterbox. But I'm afraid I haven't had a minute till now."

She rushed into the lounge returning with a white envelope.

Inside was a card, liberally sprinkled with crayon-drawn holly with a huge Santa in the middle. In Chris's handwriting it said: *To My Frend, Ed. Lov from Chris.*

Ed felt tears pricking his eyes. He could think of nothing to say. Mrs Elliot smiled and touched his hand.

"Perhaps you'd like to join us for Christmas dinner tomorrow? There'll be just the family and I'm sure Chris would be so happy to see you."

Ed nodded and managed to murmur his thanks before making his way back home. It would be nice to spend Christmas with a real family again.

It would be nice to see the boy's reaction to the bright red, wooden engine he had so painstakingly made for him.

Yes, he might just take Mrs Elliot up on her kindly offer. □

THIS lakeland walk, overleaf, is just one of the many fine features on the Stourhead estate in Wiltshire. One of the National Trust's properties, it's easy to see why lots of visitors are attracted here. There's a beautiful mansion, containing many notable works of art, which was built for a banker, Henry Hoare, in the 1720s. Some years later, Hoare's son laid out the superb pleasure gardens which are reckoned to be among the finest in England. Beside the lake are unusual buildings — like the Temple of Flora, seen here — while nearby Kingsettle Hill affords superb views of the whole area.

STOURHEAD ESTATE, Wiltshire : J CAMPBELL KERR

Good For Each Other

"MY granddaughter is coming for a holiday," Mrs MacFarlane called out to her neighbour. "That's why I've been washing all these curtains and things."

David Murray had been staring at the lines of washing billowing in the breeze and now he waved and nodded at his elderly neighbour and called back.

"Let's hope the weather stays fine, then."

But as he was driving out of the village a few seconds later it suddenly occurred to him that Mrs MacFarlane had wanted more of an answer than that. During the past five months since he had rented the cottage adjacent to hers, he hadn't got to know her too well — she was like himself, reserved and yet willing to be neighbourly as and when the occasion arose.

She had gladly accepted his offer to dig her garden in the spring, for instance. And he never hesitated to accept the odd sample of her home baking.

What he liked most about her was that she seldom asked him questions and never volunteered much information about herself. That first day when she'd handed him the key to the cottage, she'd told him simply:

"I keep a key at the lawyer's bidding. But for myself I don't believe in locked doors."

Thanking her, David had promised to return the key when he left. And she had nodded and told him:

"The house is all cleaned and prepared for you."

Now he recalled the welcoming air of the house and the bright clean curtains at the windows. And for the first time, he realised that Mrs MacFarlane must have done all the work herself.

by ELIZA YEAMAN

He braked, and as the van screeched to a halt he saw that it would be difficult to turn on the narrow road, so he reversed swiftly to a wider section of road. He was reasonably cautious but he had only part of his mind on what he was doing.

He was visualising the high windows, imagining Mrs MacFarlane climbing that rickety old step-ladder she kept in the shed. He almost saw her falling . . .

He didn't notice that he was holding his breath until he saw the curtains still on the line — naturally, since it was only a matter of minutes since he'd left.

Mrs MacFarlane heard the van returning. But still, she was surprised to hear the tap at the back door. She turned from the sink, and looked at her neighbour enquiringly.

David's face was brick red as he said awkwardly:

"I forgot something — so I had to come back."

Then he told himself he was being ridiculous. No matter how

independent and self-sufficient she was, he could not be a party to letting her act dangerously. So he took the plunge.

"Let me know when your curtains are dry, Mrs MacFarlane," he said positively, "and I'll hang them up. All right?"

Mrs MacFarlane seemed to frown, then she began to say:

"It's good of you to offer."

"But I insist," David interrupted firmly, and added quite roughly, "I shall sit on the dyke and watch them drying."

Something like a gleam came into Mrs MacFarlane's eye as she studied his face. Then she gave him a slow smile.

"Right you are then, Mr Murray," she said. "And if I don't see you on the dyke I'll give you a shout, will I? When they are dry."

David nodded and turned to go. For no reason that he could fathom he knew she was amused.

Well, I don't care, he thought. I'd rather she laughed at me than fall off that ladder. And just to make sure, he removed the ladder from where it was propped near her door.

He set it firmly against his own wall before he went inside to fetch a book to read while he kept his vigil. The ancient abbey ruins which he had planned to photograph this morning could easily wait until tomorrow.

INSIDE her kitchen, Mrs MacFarlane was drying her hands thoughtfully. She felt a little bit guilty. Obviously the lad imagined she was foolish enough to risk going up a ladder.

She ought to have told him that Billy Mearns, the postman, had taken down the curtains — and she had intended to ask Tom who drove the butcher's van to put them up tomorrow, since the postman might not be back this way for a while.

She could have explained all that to David Murray. But she hadn't. A movement outside caught her eye and she nodded to herself. There he was perched up on the dyke and that cold, withdrawn expression was back on his face.

Mrs MacFarlane searched through the top drawer of her dresser until she found her spectacles and the letter she had received from her lawyer about David Murray renting the cottage.

. . . *I know that you told me you did not want a new tenant. But as it is now some years since your cousin passed away, I trust that time has healed your sorrow and I beg you to consider allowing my young friend to lease the premises for a limited period, initially six months, if you are agreeable.*

Without breaking any confidences, I can tell you that David Murray has suffered a great personal tragedy. He has asked me to find accommodation for him where he can be completely isolated . . .

Mrs MacFarlane folded the letter. She'd written back, saying yes, and a day or two later James Smeaton, her elderly lawyer, had come to visit her. He told her more about David Murray, whose girlfriend had died in a fire a few days before the wedding.

Mrs MacFarlane was no great believer in solitude as a means of curing grief. But she had kept her opinion to herself, although she had reluctantly consented to write and inform James Smeaton if the young man showed any signs of becoming a danger to himself.

"His parents are afraid that he won't bother to cook for himself and wash his clothes and so on — but I believe he will," James Smeaton had said. "I'm inclined to agree with him that he needs to get away from his present surroundings."

Up to now, Mrs MacFarlane thought, the lawyer had been right. The lad did look after himself. But he had no social life at all. In fact, Mrs MacFarlane believed — until today — that he had turned in on himself, that he noticed nothing of what went on outside his own misery. But now . . .? There he was sitting out there on the dyke grimly determined to save an old woman climbing a step-ladder. That had to be a good sign.

Before she took off her glasses, she decided to have another wee read of the letter from Doreen, her granddaughter. If David Murray is on his way to a cure, Mrs MacFarlane smiled to herself, Doreen will be the very one to help him along.

Even in a letter, her cheeky bubbling personality could not be repressed.

> . . . *see you on Friday then, Gran darling, and don't forget that small is beautiful and I don't want to get fat! So keep the scones and fruit cake to a minimum if you happen to be baking for me coming.*

But Doreen's letter wasn't a true reflection of her present frame of mind. From the moment she arrived, her grandmother saw that she was putting a brave face on some inward heartache.

H ONESTLY, Gran, you can read me like a book." Doreen smiled as the old woman began to question her. Then she sighed.

"I don't really want to talk about it . . . you see, I had a quarrel with someone . . ."

She bit her lip and there was a glint of tears in her eyes as she confessed, "I was the one to blame . . . so if I'm unhappy it's entirely my own fault. And I just want to forget the whole thing."

Mrs MacFarlane patted her hand comfortingly.

"Well, I won't plague you with questions, my lamb. But I'm warning you — I want to see roses in those cheeks of yours before the week is out. Good food and plenty of fresh air is what you need."

"And I've come to the right place," Doreen agreed, adding, "tomorrow I shall start with a long hike through the glen."

"You'll be needing some sandwiches then," her grandmother said, "and a flask of tea."

Next morning Doreen set out, pretending to groan under the weight of the picnic her grandmother had packed into her haversack.

From his window, David Murray saw the girl laughing as she turned at the edge of the path to wave.

So that's the granddaughter, he thought, recalling some of the things the old woman had told him about the girl. And later, when he had finished hanging the curtains, Mrs MacFarlane had shown him a snapshot of a smiling, dark-haired, dark-eyed girl.

Pretty as a picture — the words drifted through his mind as he strained to catch a last glimpse of her. But no, the photograph doesn't do her justice, he decided, she is beautiful . . .

Then he turned swiftly away from the window and collected his photographic gear and his notebook. Yesterday he had resolved to avoid the girl as far as possible. He would be wise to stick to that decision, he told himself.

No doubt the old woman would tell the girl that he was extremely busy now, compiling an illustrated guide to the history of the area.

★　　★　　★　　★

During the first week of Doreen's holiday, she met and spoke to David Murray on a number of occasions.

But he made no impression on her — Mrs MacFarlane was certain of that — and she was a little bit disappointed, too. Because she had a strong feeling that if only they could get to know each other better, the young pair would be good for each other.

On the first day of her second week, Doreen was kept indoors by the torrential rain which fell until early evening. It had been a long day, she thought, as she put on her wellington boots and ventured out into the grey drizzle.

Her grandmother was not in the least talkative but she seemed to expect Doreen to keep up a constant flow of chatter. And when there was silence, Doreen always became conscious of a certain intent, gently-enquiring look on her grandmother's face.

Yes, today has been more tiring than any of my long treks, Doreen thought, as she splashed her way through the puddles on the track which led away from the back of the buildings.

She had no definite route in mind, she didn't even realise that she was heading for the fairy pool, until she found herself at the edge of the rushing burn, watching the water foaming into the pool and then running out again into the narrow burn.

And while she gazed, there was an oddly-fearful fluttering in her heart. Shall I make a wish? Dare I . . . ?

"It's quite fascinating, isn't it?"

Doreen was startled to hear David Murray's voice. He was standing only a few feet away.

"I didn't mean to scare you," David said.

"That's all right," she answered. But although he had moved nearer to her, she still had to raise her voice to make herself heard.

He couldn't possibly have known what I was thinking, Doreen assured herself — unless he also had come here to make a wish. She turned her head to glance at him curiously. Then she blushed again as their eyes met and she realised that he had been staring at her.

"We may as well walk back together," David shouted against the noise of the burn. At the same time he pulled up the hood of his jacket and indicated ruefully that the rain was becoming heavier by the second.

Doreen nodded and started to follow him. Then she changed her mind and went to gaze deeply into the pool.

I wish . . . I do truly wish that I had never quarrelled with Stuart . . .

DAVID was watching her with a slightly-puzzled frown on his face. And as they walked away from the enchanted place, Doreen suddenly didn't mind telling him.

"I always make a wish. I believe in the magic of the fairy pool."

"You do? But why?" David asked with an amused smile.

"It's a family tradition," Doreen told him with a grin. "My sister and brothers and I discovered the pool when we were children. We were quite overawed by the whole atmosphere of the crazy water and the mad whirlpool. We were town kids — not at all accustomed to the wonders of nature."

"But it's not a natural pool," David told her. "It was man made — there are quite a few of them in the district. About six hundred years ago, the monks from the abbey went out in groups to build wells — I haven't precisely discovered why yet. I've come across one or two theories . . ."

"Stop!" Doreen pleaded. "You are shattering my illusions! I refuse

▶*over*

they were first...

IF it hadn't been for Alexander Graham Bell, the telephone might never have been invented and the instrument never have become the indispensable household item we use so freely today.

It was 'way back in 1876 that this Scots-born physicist relayed that first momentous telephone message. At the time, he was working on teaching methods for deaf-mutes when his research led him to his fantastic invention.

to give up my faith in the powers of our fairy pool."

David smiled at her. He couldn't seem to help smiling at her.

"Perhaps you're right. Maybe the place does have some sort of magical power. Who knows?"

Then, as the cottages came into view, he offered impulsively, "I could take you to see the other pools, one especially is quite impressive."

Doreen agreed to go with him next day. She told her grandmother about her meeting with David and gave a satisfyingly detailed account of their conversation.

The following morning Mrs MacFarlane watched the young pair driving off.

"I knew it. Didn't I just know that they ought to be together!" she said to herself happily.

★　　★　　★　　★

The day was bright and clear — ideal for a tour around some of the historic sites which David was eager to show Doreen.

His enthusiasm was infectious and Doreen was soon convinced that the pools had indeed been built by men. But she didn't allow David to become too smug, especially when he asked her to pose for his camera above one of the pools.

"I suppose you'll need a live model to make your pictures less boring." Doreen gave him a cheeky grin as she obligingly moved towards the stone platform which he had indicated.

Later, when they stopped at a grassy bank for a picnic lunch, David said to her with admiring humour:

"You were right about your face improving my photographs, Doreen. And you improve this scene, too."

"No photos of the monkey while she is eating." Doreen bit into a sandwich. "It's an invasion of privacy."

"One thing I like about you." David laughed. "You are so quick with these snappy answers!"

"I have two brothers," Doreen retorted. "I've had to learn to defend myself and give as good as I get."

"My sister used to tease me . . ." David began, then halted abruptly, his smile fading.

The look of stark tragedy on his face affected Doreen profoundly. She was compelled to ask him:

"Did something . . . happen to your sister?"

"No — it happened to me," David answered in a low voice filled with bitterness. Then his chin lifted as if he'd been hit and a spasm of consternation crossed his face.

"That's not true — it didn't happen to me — nothing happened to me." Suddenly he covered his face with his hands. "I can't believe I've been so selfish."

Watching his bowed head and slumped shoulders, Doreen reached out to put a sympathetic hand on his arm.

"I'm sure you are being too hard on yourself," she said softly.

"You don't give me the impression that you are selfish . . . silent, yes. I've noticed that about you."

When he still didn't look up, she gave his arm a little squeeze. "Come on, David, talk to me about it. Bottling up your emotions is never any good — and talking to a stranger often helps."

He took his hands away from his face.

"I don't feel as if you are a stranger." Then he paused, looking away from her again before he continued, "I've never spoken to anyone about this . . ."

IN a flat voice devoid of all emotion, he began to describe the girl he had been planning to marry. Then he went on to give a factual account of the fire in which she had died and her parents had been injured.

Only when he came to the end of his narrative did his voice break.

"I didn't give a thought to her parents, nor anyone else . . . I've been so wrapped up in my own grief."

"That was natural." Doreen was holding his hand now, and she consoled him quietly and sincerely. "You had a right to mourn, David. I understand that and I'm certain everyone who knows you must also understand."

"Thanks, Doreen." David spoke gratefully but his eyes were brooding and morose.

On the drive home, he scarcely volunteered a word and it was obvious that he had to make a big effort to answer any remark of Doreen's. But she didn't mind, for she was preoccupied with her own thoughts . . .

Mrs MacFarlane was sitting alone that evening when she heard David's footsteps and his timid knock at the door.

"Doreen has gone along to the telephone box," she told the young man. "She said she'd take a walk round by her fairy pool after she made her phone call."

"Right — thanks — I'll find her!"

Mrs MacFarlane stood at the door with her lips pursed and a baffled frown on her face as he disappeared into the distance. Doreen had given her such a big hug before she went out. And she'd said solemnly:

"Wish me luck, Gran. I'm about to make the most important phone call of my entire life."

David caught up with Doreen before she arrived at the fairy pool.

"I wanted to thank you . . ." David was out of breath as he walked behind her along the narrow path.

She smiled at him over her shoulder. But she wasn't in a mood for talking. She was glad that the roar of the water made normal speech impossible as she reached the pool.

They stood together, gazing in fascinated wonder at the swirling waters. But Doreen was aware of a great sense of peace in her own heart — a serenity which contrasted strangely with her pleasure in the confusion of the whirlpool below her feet.

David moved closer to her. He also was conscious of an inner tranquillity. At last he had come to terms with his sorrow and he associated his new-found peace of mind with this lovely girl . . .

Now they turned to each other and he put his arms around her. She raised her face to his and he saw a faintly perplexed look in her eyes as he bent his head to kiss her. It was a tender kiss but she didn't put her arms around him, and her lips were cool.

David gazed at her questioningly and she gave him a small smile which conveyed regret mingled with gentle understanding. Then she took his hand and led him away from the turmoil of the roaring water.

"I want to thank you, David," she said to him. "You made me realise that there is no such thing as magic. It was childish and stupid of me to believe that making a wish would give me back my true love."

She tilted her head to look at him. "I didn't think I had it in me to say I was wrong and to ask for forgiveness — but it was easy after all."

David was puzzled. "That phone call you made . . . ?"

She nodded, and her face was suddenly lit by an inner radiance.

"Stuart is . . ." She sighed as she answered softly, ". . . the most wonderful person."

David smiled. He was happy for her and yet he was aware of a sensation of regret as he told her quietly:

"You are a wonderful person, too, Doreen — I hope we shall meet again someday."

MRS MACFARLANE decided to sit outside in the sun the following afternoon. Maybe the fresh air will help me to make sense of it all, she thought.

"You'll come to my wedding now, Granny darling. Won't you?" Doreen had pleaded, her eyes shining as she hurried to get a lift from the postman so that she could catch the Glasgow bus.

An hour or so later, David Murray had brought back the key to the cottage. And he had told her happily:

"I've had enough of the solitary life, Mrs MacFarlane. I've decided to go home to my family again."

Mrs MacFarlane closed her eyes. So you were wrong about them making a match of it, she told herself sternly. Yet she couldn't help thinking that they were good for each other. It isn't good to be alone, she told herself.

Then she opened her eyes and sat up straight. Wasn't that what her family and her lawyer had been telling her for years and she had refused to listen!

Before she could change her mind, she went inside and wrote to the lawyer asking him to find a new tenant for the empty cottage. She knew that she could rely on him to send someone suitable.

She liked her solitude. But it would be fine to know that there was somebody next door. □

by JEAN
McDOUGALL

A NEW BEGINNING

MID morning, in the tiny florist shop she ran with her friend and partner, Hilary, Louise Barr announced, "I have to go to the police station. Got a card this morning."

"I always knew they'd catch up with you sometime!" Hilary laughed, looking up from the bouquet she had been working on. "But when you're there, give my love to Brian."

"I thought he had that already." Louise was rummaging desperately in a large hold-all in pursuit of the card she had been requested to bring with her.

"I expect it'll be about the watch I handed in quite some time ago," she added.

"Oh, I remember," Hilary said. "It's a little beauty, too. I suppose it's been claimed and they want to hand over a reward to the finder. Where will we go to celebrate?"

"I think we'd better wait to see how much it is. Oh, here's the card at last. I'll be on my way, Hilary. Will be back just as soon as I can."

"I'll manage. Most of the orders are ready for the van when Steve comes by. Off you go and enjoy yourself."

"In the police station? Some hope!"

It was a brisk November day with a clear blue sky and a fresh wind that ruffled her brown curls as she set off at a good pace for the station. The beat constable spotted her at once and came up to the desk grinning.

"Hi! Come to confess, have you?"

"Oh, Brian. I've already been through all that with Hilary. She sends you her love, by the way."

A small spasm of envy hit her as she saw the way his eyes lit up on hearing Hilary's name. Louise had lots of friends and had fancied herself as being in love several times, but she was aware that none of her romances had come anywhere near the feelings Brian and Hilary had for each other.

"Well, what can we do for you? Oh, you've a card there."

With a smiling "Excuse me," he took it from her and disappeared into a private room nearby. Seconds later, he was behind the counter again with a tiny gold watch in his big palm.

Louise stared. "You mean no-one has claimed it — an expensive watch like that?"

"So it would seem."

"But I can't . . ." She shook her head as he passed the watch and a receipt book across the desk to her.

"You're the owner now, Louise, so if you would just sign your name on the line there."

"But, Brian, this is all wrong. There must be someone somewhere breaking her heart over losing it. I can't leave it at that. What do you think I should do?"

He shrugged his wide shoulders.

"Well, if you're dead set on finding the owner, you could try an ad in the Lost and Found coloumns," he said, "but chances are it was dropped by a visitor who's gone home.

"Actually, we've a drawerful of watches that have been handed in, along with an odd-ball collection of anything else you care to mention. Is Hilary coping on her own right now?"

"Yes." Nodding, she scribbled her name on the receipt and seconds later, she was out in the wintry sunshine again, clutching the watch in one hand, as though it was a butterfly that might escape if she didn't take care.

B ACK at the shop, Hilary produced a magnifying glass so that they could study the inscription inside. *To Minta*, it read, and there was a date about two years ago.

"It's beautiful," Hilary enthused. "I wonder who she was."

"And where she is now. Brian suggested an ad. in the local paper. What would you do?"

"I'd keep it." Hilary was always practical. "Why spend money on an advertisement when it's been lying in police custody all these months? Surely that would be the first place the owner would try, once she discovered it was gone? You found it in a litter bin, didn't you?"

"Not *in*, underneath."

Louise shook a reproving head at her friend, resenting the implication that she was in the habbit of rifling through the rubbish. She had been waiting for a bus one day in the summer when something glinting attracted her eye near the kerb.

"Minta," Hilary was saying reflectively. "It's not a very common name, is it? I'm trying to remember . . . didn't we have an order some weeks ago for someone with a name like that?"

"Did we?" Louise was instantly alert and had the order book open on the counter in an instant.

"Don't suppose you remember the surname, do you?"

Hilary didn't, and went off to make them both a cup of coffee, while Louise pored over the entries, some almost illegible in her friend's scribble.

"How's it going?" Hilary asked a few minutes later.

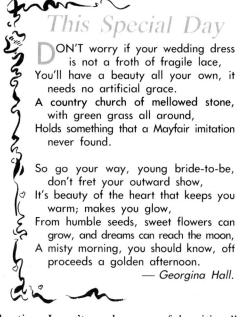

This Special Day

DON'T worry if your wedding dress
is not a froth of fragile lace,
You'll have a beauty all your own, it
needs no artificial grace.
A country church of mellowed stone,
with green grass all around,
Holds something that a Mayfair imitation
never found.

So go your way, young bride-to-be,
don't fret your outward show,
It's beauty of the heart that keeps you
warm; makes you glow,
From humble seeds, sweet flowers can
grow, and dreams can reach the moon,
A misty morning, you should know, off
proceeds a golden afternoon.
— *Georgina Hall.*

"Oh, it's hopeless. Half the time I can't read your awful writing." Hilary paused in the act of spooning sugar into the cups.

"I remember now — it was to be delivered on July the twenty-third — the same day as the Royal Wedding."

Turning the pages over quickly, Louise spotted it at last.

"You're right, Hilary. A Mrs Minta Fleming — and her address is here, too. I found the watch not far from where she lives.

Oh, great! I'll go and see her on the way home tonight!"

★   ★   ★   ★

The address turned out to be a tenement with a controlled entry inter-com at the closemouth, but no names on the buttons. Louise had to press a couple at random before she got a reply and was then directed to buzz one of the buttons on the top row.

"Hello, Mrs Fleming?"

The answering voice was very soft, and she guessed it belonged to an elderly woman who naturally was reluctant to give admission to a stranger.

"I'm from the shop that delivered a bouquet of flowers to you last July — the day of the Royal Wedding. Perhaps you remember."

"Yes?"

"May I come up and see you for a few minutes?"

"Yes, if you wish."

Mrs Fleming was looking over the banisters as Louise climbed the long flights of stairs. Louise smiled up at her reassuringly.

"I'm so sorry to disturb you, Mrs Fleming, but I've come to see if you lost a watch — perhaps about May or June of this year?"

The thin elderly lady looked somewhat flustered, but she invited the girl into her rather old-fashioned flat.

"A watch? I don't think so, but then my memory isn't as good as it used to be. Please sit down, won't you?"

Louise produced the watch.

"This is it — and it has your name inscribed in it. I found it, you see, and it's been in the police station ever since. It's really a lucky coincidence that we had a note of your name in our shop. My partner remembered the very nice gentleman who called to order flowers for you."

"My son," Mrs Fleming said with pride. "Would you like a cup of tea, my dear?"

"No, please don't go to any trouble. I just wanted to return the watch to its rightful owner, and as I have another appointment this evening, I'd better be on my way."

"Then I'm afraid you must take the watch with you," the older woman said, smiling. "I never had such a watch. It's really lovely, but it is not mine. Thank you, though, for thinking of me."

Later, Louise phoned Hilary with the promised report.

"Oh dear. What a wasted journey. What's the next step?"

"Well, I've phoned in an ad for the Lost and Found columns, with my number. We'll just have to wait and see."

THERE were some responses, but either the inscriptions or the descriptions did not fit, and nobody mentioned the word "Minta."

Louise was ready to give up when there was an early-morning call from a building company.

"Hold the line," said a clipped young voice. "I have a call for you."

Then a man spoke, pithily to the point.

"You're wasting your money with that ad," he told her. "The watch has no owner."

"Who is this?" she began, and heard the click of disconnection.

Undeterred, she looked up the building firm in the phone book, dialled the operator, and asked who put the call through to her number.

"That must have been Frank," she heard the telephonists discussing the matter between them. Then into the phone,

"Hello, miss. You were probably speaking to Frank Duncan, but he's not here right now — he's one of our site foremen."

"I'd very much like to see him about the phone call," she explained, "so if you could tell me which site he's working on today, I'd be really grateful."

Armed with the address, Louise set out during her lunch hour, promising Hilary she'd be back by two o'clock, at the latest.

"Take your time," her friend said. "Frank Duncan might turn out to be Mr Wonderful."

"Not the way he sounded on the phone this morning! Mr Horrible was more like it."

The site was out in the suburbs, but luckily a bus took her to the terminus and from there, it was a few minutes' walk, though she thanked her lucky stars the weather was dry, otherwise she could have been trudging through sticky clay and mud.

Some workmen pointed out the site office to her, and when she knocked on the door, it was opened by a good-looking young man with blond hair and twinkling eyes.

"May I help you, I hope," he began, grinning.

"Mr Frank Duncan?"

"Try Eric Carpenter. It sounds better — at least I think so." With a courtly gesture, he waved her to a wooden stool. "Have a seat. He should be back soon. Like a cuppa?"

"Er, no . . . thanks all the same. Can you tell me what he's like?"

"Frank? Oh, he's OK. A bit peppery when he's tearing a strip off us — the work force, I mean — but a really good foreman. Very fair."

His eyes swept over her appreciatively. "You don't know him then?"

She shrugged. "We exchanged — no, that's wrong. I got about a dozen words from him over the phone before he cut me off."

"That's Frank Duncan. Short and to the point."

"Short and extremely rude."

Suddenly Louise was aware that a third party had entered the site office, and one glance at the man's stern face told her it was the foreman.

Suddenly ill at ease, she stammered, "You . . . you rang me this morning — about a watch I advertised with a note of the date inside."

"I don't know how you managed to trace me, young woman, but I thought I made it quite, quite clear that no-one would be claiming it. I also said you were wasting your money putting advertisements in the papers."

"Well, thank you, but I've brought it to you, since it's obviously yours."

She held the watch out to him, then recoiled at the fury in his face.

"Will you get out of here, and take that — that object with you? I never want to see it again — or you!"

LOUISE was about to make a spirited reply, when she found her arm being taken gently by Eric Carpenter.

"Let's go," he whispered urgently.

Moments later she was outside, glad of the breeze cooling her hot cheeks and equally appreciative of the firm arm round her waist.

"He's having a bit of a rough time of it right now," Eric was trying to explain as he walked her towards a temporary car park. "Lots of things going wrong on site, and he has to carry the can with the bosses."

"We all have our problems," she retorted. "That hardly gives him the right to be so downright rude, and without any real cause that I can see."

"Look, here's my car. Let me run you back to wherever you were going, and I'll try to put you in the picture about Frank."

'What about your job?" she asked uncertainly. "I wouldn't like to be responsible for turning all that bad temper in your direction!"

He grinned as he helped her into the front seat of the small runabout.

"It wouldn't be the first time," Eric Carpenter said. "Truly, I've had my share of Frank's temper — we all have, and most of the time we deserve it."

"Does that go for me, too?"

"No, you couldn't be expected to know the story behind the watch. Frank told me once about Minta — they were going to be married, but at the last minute almost, she called it off. She'd fallen for someone else, so she gave him back the gifts he'd given her.

"I think he sold most of them, but the watch with her name in it, he threw away. Do you see now why he didn't want it back?"

As they sat waiting for the lights changing, she said quietly, "Yes, I understand a bit better now, and I'm sorry for him. It must have been so hurtful having it all stirred up again."

"My sister has a book on names," Eric said with a quick sideways look before returning his gaze to the road ahead. "I looked up Minta once, and ironically, in this case, it means *remembered with love*."

"Do you think Mr Duncan might ever change his mind about wanting the watch back?" she said after a while.

"Not in a million years. My turn to ask a question now — do you think you might consider coming out with me some evening you're free?"

"Sounds fun," she said, dimpling. "My friend and I run a flower shop together. You can get me at this number, if you want to."

"Indeed I do. How about tonight?"

"No," she said consideringly. "There's something I have to do this evening, but if tomorrow suits you."

"Pick you up at the shop at six-ish? We can have a meal and take in a show."

"I'll look forward to it, Eric." She got out of the car with a final, "Thanks for the lift."

There was plenty to tell Hilary about, including her plan for this particular evening when she intended calling again on Mrs Fleming and presenting her with the watch.

After all, it did have her name on it, and even on short acquaintance, it was plain to see that she was one of the chosen people who would be remembered with love. □

they were first...

WHEN he lined up with pacemakers Chris Brasher and Chris Chataway at Oxford in May 1954, only one thing was in Roger Bannister's mind. He was determined to be first to run the mile in under four minutes.

The athletes set off at a cracking pace, and with little more than 200 yards to go, Bannister swept past Chataway to make his bid. Close to exhaustion, he crossed the line . . . the watch was stopped . . . 3 min. 59·4 sec. — he had done it!

THE weather was more than suited to the occasion the day Myra
Findlay moved into the village. It was the first really calm day
the inhabitants of Little Craigton had seen that spring, so most
of them were in their gardens enjoying the sunshine while it lasted.

It was just as well, really, otherwise they might never have seen
Mrs Findlay drive up to Rose Cottage in her neat, blue Mini, nor
witnessed the prompt arrival of the furniture van at half past two.

The men Mrs Findlay had hired were punctual, polite and efficient,
and the entire operation was carried out to her satisfaction in less
than an hour. When it was all over, the removal men drove off, the
door was closed behind her and, except for the blue car at the front
gate, there was nothing to show for the afternoon's activities.

That Nuisance Next Door!

by CHRISTINE NICOLSON

It was quite a different story two months later when Ben Morrison breezed into Little Craigton — rather like the wind that was howling down Main Street that day! It was a morning for sitting by the fireside and, judging by the empty streets, that's what most people were doing.

But Ben's arrival soon changed that! As his old, yellow car spluttered, coughed and banged its way up Main Street, the noise brought faces to windows. A few brave souls even ventured out to their front doors!

The commotion only stopped when Ben's old banger came to a halt outside Briar Cottage, and was parked neatly beside Mrs Findlay's blue Mini.

Ben climbed out and patted his car affectionately on the bonnet.

"You did well, Tilly, my lass." He grinned. "You got us here, although you nearly fell to pieces in the process. Still, you can have a rest now. We won't be going far for quite a while!"

He paused and looked around, beaming broadly. His new home! What a marvellous feeling! A real home of his own after all those years at sea.

Catching sight of a man standing on the pavement a few houses down, he called a cheery greeting before turning to his own garden gate.

By the time the removal men arrived twenty minutes later, Ben had unpacked the car, passed the time of day with his new neighbour and put the kettle on to boil.

The flitting kept the villagers talking for months! The wonderful array of treasures that were unloaded from the old van were of a kind seldom seen in Little Craigton.

Ben's travels round the world had amassed all kinds of curiosities, and he laughed and joked with the removal men as oddity after oddity was carried into the house. And soon, despite the awful weather, quite a crowd had gathered on the pavement to watch the proceedings.

The whole thing took much longer than necessary, but no-one seemed to mind, and half past five saw Ben, the removal men and Jim Cummings — the widower from three doors down — tucking into egg and chips, which Ben had rustled up from seemingly nowhere.

"Oh, yes, I've been used to looking out for myself," Ben told his new friend when the removal men had finally gone. "I've been on my own a long time now."

"Well, I think you cope pretty well," Jim said in admiration.

"But do you know something, Jim?" Ben said thoughtfully. "I've been too long alone — I think I'll get a companion!"

YOU could say it was dislike at first sight! When Myra Findlay looked out of her kitchen window and saw Horatio, Ben's new kitten, digging up the ground around her favourite rose bush, she let out a gasp of dismay.

"Shoo, shoo!" she cried, rushing out in time to see the culprit disappear into the wilderness that was Ben's garden next door.

On the second day, Horatio was seen unearthing some daffodil bulbs and playfully pit-patting them across the newly-mown lawn.

By day five he had systematically worked his way down the garden and had now arrived at the beautiful peony rose Myra had just planted.

Enough was enough! Indignation written all over her face, she marched round to Ben's front door and pressed firmly on the bell.

Ben's smile withered when he opened the door and saw her frozen look.

"Mr . . ." She peered at the nameplate. "Mr Morrison, your cat is ruining my flower beds. Unlike some people, I have worked hard in my garden and am proud of it. I won't have it ruined by a careless man who can't keep his animal under control. Kindly keep your cat on your own side of the wall in future! Good day."

Ben's jaw dropped. Did that ill-natured woman really think he could make Horatio do what he wanted? Everyone knew cats were a law unto themselves. They were free spirits — you couldn't tie them down. That was one of the reasons he liked them so much — he was a bit like that!

Cats are also creatures of habit, and as was his habit, Horatio found himself in Mrs Findlay's garden the following morning, lured there by a flighty sparrow. It led him a merry dance, right up an elm tree, in fact!

Then, when the kitten had climbed as high as he could possibly go, the sparrow flew away. Poor Horatio! No way up and no way down. And nothing to be gained for his trouble either!

Soon his pitiful mewing had attracted quite an audience, and there was a good deal of noise. The noise, however, didn't quite reach Myra Findlay. She was in her front room beside the fire, listening to a concert on the radio.

Ben, in his kitchen trying to come to grips with the gardening manual he'd borrowed from Jim Cummings — he really must do something about the mess out the back — was gradually alerted to the fact that there was something amiss.

Ten minutes later, her concert over, Myra emerged just in time to see Ben climb up, reach out for Horatio, break a branch off the tree and send it crashing through her greenhouse roof!

Horatio, meanwhile, using Ben as a ladder, jumped quickly to safety and disappeared into the undergrowth next door.

Harsh words followed. Ben was apologetic, willing to pay for the damage — and finally, seeing the funny side of it, was so consumed with laughter that it was all he could do to straighten up and clamber back over the garden wall!

The cheque she received did little to calm Mrs Findlay's agitation, and although Ben always greeted her with a smile and a pleasant word afterwards, she never spoke to him. She continued to clear up the mess Horatio still caused from time to time, but she never looked Ben's way as he struggled with his shambles of a garden.

"I'd like to be friends with her," Ben told Jim one morning. "I'm not the kind of bloke to hold a grudge, and it bothers me being on bad terms with a neighbour. But she won't even look at me!"

"Never mind," Jim sympathised. "If you ask me, she's not worth the worry. You're better off out of it!"

THE months passed as months do in small villages. Spring sales were followed by summer fêtes and jumble sales. Then in November the whole community was talking about the coming social evening in the village hall.

Myra Findlay went along rather under duress. It wasn't her kind of thing at all, but she'd been talked into it by the very persuasive postmistress, who'd made her feel she'd be conspicuous by her absence!

But I don't really get on with people, she told herself on the day of the social. She looked in the mirror, trying to decide what to wear. A pleasant face, spoiled by sad, expressionless eyes, stared back at her. I've never been much good at mixing, she thought.

When Duncan was killed, she'd retreated into herself for a time, and somehow life had never really got under way for her again. Oh, she'd lived a full enough life, but it had never been quite what it should have . . .

She looked at the photograph she always kept on her bedside table. She and Duncan had been so happy on their wedding day, and didn't he look smart in his uniform? Just eighteen short months they'd had . . .

Myra felt a tear come to her eye. Last week had been the anniversary of his death — this was always a bad time of year for her . . .

Oh, really, this was so silly! A lot of years had passed since then. She must pull herself together!

That evening Myra made her way to the village hall. She found a quiet seat in a corner beside elderly Mrs MacDougall, one of the few people whose acquaintance she'd allowed herself to make since her arrival in the village.

Gradually the hall filled up and the band began to play. The vicar, doing the rounds, came over to join her.

"Oh, don't you just love these old songs, Mrs Findlay?" he said. "Those war songs were really special, don't you think? Remember how wonderful it was when we all worked together — what a marvellous community spirit there was then? Family and friends all helped each other out."

Myra nodded. "Yes, I know what you mean."

She didn't know what she would have done without her friends and family when Duncan was killed in action.

Memories flooded back as the band played all the old familiar tunes. She and Duncan had been so in love. There had only ever been Duncan for her. They had loved dancing and had spent their last night together at a dance. Then he'd gone the next day and had never returned . . .

Myra had literally changed overnight, cutting herself off from the real world. So much time wasted without Duncan . . .

Then gradually she'd emerged from her grief. The numbness left her and she began to enjoy life again. But no-one had ever been able to take her husband's place . . .

A voice broke into her thoughts.

"Would you care to dance?"

M YRA FINDLAY looked up in astonishment. Ben Morrison, her tiresome neighbour!

"I really don't think . . ." She hesitated and looked around her.

The minister and Mrs MacDougall were looking at her expectantly. It would be churlish to refuse. It wouldn't be right . . . What would they think?

She stood up and Ben led her on to the floor. The music started up again — but conversation didn't. Myra was much too angry and embarrassed to speak!

Then suddenly she became aware of the music — "Thanks For The Memory." That so-very-special song . . .

On that last night they'd been together, she and Duncan, it had been played at the dance, and for some unfathomable reason of his own Duncan had held tighter than ever before. It was as if he knew — as if some instinct was telling him he would never be back. They'd left the dance shortly after. That was the last dance they'd ever had together . . .

And now here she was, dancing one more time to that same special tune. It was almost like stepping back in time. If she closed her eyes . . .

A lump came to her throat. Oh, no! This was too much! Surely she wasn't going to cry? She thought she'd cried all her tears years ago! Strange how a piece of music could remind you . . .

The tears began to slowly trickle down her cheeks, and she fumbled as she brushed them away.

"Why, Mrs Findlay, you're upset," Ben said gently.

In Our Dreams

WE all have dreams; some fade like
dying flowers,
But they provide their share of gilded
hours,
In threads of gold they weave a pattern
fair,
The wealth of all the world is yours to
share.

A spider web of dreams is all you need,
Reality may blossom from the seed,
An added bonus then you gain from life
A compensation for every hour of
strife.

— *Georgina Hall.*

77

Myra lowered her eyes as she struggled to compose herself.

"It's just the music," she muttered.

"I think you should sit down." Ben took command and led her over to a table in a quiet corner at the back of the hall.

"Here you are," he said kindly, pulling out a chair for her. "Can I help?" he went on. "You're not ill or anything, are you?"

Myra shook her head.

"No, really. I'll be fine . . . Thank you," she said, the catch in her voice betraying the embarrassment she felt.

Ben looked at her helplessly.

"I don't know what to say," he said. "I'm not used to ladies crying." He smiled awkwardly. "My dancing wasn't that bad, was it?" he joked.

Myra looked up at him and smiled in spite of herself.

"Not at all, Mr Morrison. You were very good, in fact."

"My mother always said I had two left feet . . ."

They lapsed into silence, Ben not sure what to say, Myra still trying desperately to compose herself. At last she felt able to speak.

"I feel I owe you an explanation, Mr Morrison."

"Oh, it doesn't matter." Ben waived her words aside.

"Yes, it does," Myra insisted. "I'm sorry I made a fool of myself like that. It was just that song, 'Thanks For The Memory.' Well, it's rather special. It rather took me by surprise — I haven't danced to it for years.

"You see, my husband — Duncan — he was killed in action . . ." She smiled wistfully. "It was the last song we ever danced to. I think he almost knew . . ."

"I see." Ben nodded. "Yes, I think I understand."

HESITANT at first, Myra went on to tell him about Duncan and the short time they'd had together. Gradually her confidence grew and her shyness faded.

"You'd think I'd be over it by now," she concluded with a small smile. "But obviously not. It's a bad time for me this — last week was the anniversary of his death. It always seems worse then."

"I can imagine it does," Ben said kindly. "But you know, Mrs Findlay, you're one of the lucky ones."

"Me? Lucky?"

"Yes."

"I wouldn't have said so."

"Maybe not. But look at it this way — at least you had Duncan for those eighteen months, short though they were. Me?" He laughed in an ironic kind of way.

"Well, I've been all over the world, and I've enjoyed my life, don't get me wrong. I've hundreds of friends — making friends comes very easily to me. But do you know, in all those countries I've been to, and amongst all those friends, there's never been one really special person in my life, and that's something I've always regretted."

"I've never thought of it that way before," Myra admitted. "I only ever really saw how awful it was to have lost my husband — not how wonderful it was to have had him!"

She looked at him thoughtfully.

"Thanks, Mr Morrison . . ."

"Ben!"

"Ben." Myra smiled. "Thanks, Ben. You're a very understanding man. I feel much better now."

"Good." Ben smiled, delighted. "I'm glad I could help. Oh, listen!" There was a twinkle in his eye. "I think they're playing our tune!"

The band had struck up again. Myra started to listen and a slow smile spread over her face.

" 'It's a lovely day tomorrow,' " she sang. "Oh, Ben, you're a tonic! But," she said, a new awareness in her voice, "I'm afraid I haven't been a very good neighbour to you. Can you forgive me? Can we be friends?"

"I'd like that." Ben held out his hand and Myra grasped it. "Fighting is so pointless, don't you think? But there are two conditions to our friendship." He smiled.

"And they are?"

"One, that we go dancing on a regular basis! You really are very good, you know."

Myra blushed. "I used to dance a lot. And the other?"

"That you show me what on earth I should do to get my garden looking as good as yours! I've been too long at sea to be much good on the land!"

"It's a deal!" Myra agreed, laughing, as Ben twirled her round the dance floor.

"But I warn you, you'll be seeing a lot of me in future — that garden of yours needs an awful lot of work," she said.

"That's quite all right with me." Ben grinned. "There's nothing I'd like better."

And these particular events kept the inhabitants of Little Craigton talking right up until Christmas! □

by MARY LEDGWAY

IF YOUR HEART KNOWS

R OSS, I'm not sure enough! I . . ."

"But, Marie! I thought you loved me? That it was all settled and we would marry one day."

"I'm sorry! I thought so myself but now . . . Well, I need more time. Marriage is for ever, Ross — at least that is how I want my marriage to be, and suddenly I feel uncertain. I do care for you, but is caring enough? Give me more time, Ross, please?"

Ross Ashley looked down at the girl beside him. Her grey eyes were full of remorse as she pleaded with him. He ran his fingers gently through her long fair hair.

He had been so sure that Marie would agree to becoming engaged on his twenty-first birthday, three months away. Now he felt as though his world had just been turned upside down.

In her turn Marie felt as though she didn't know herself. Until now she had been so sure she would say yes when Ross asked her to marry

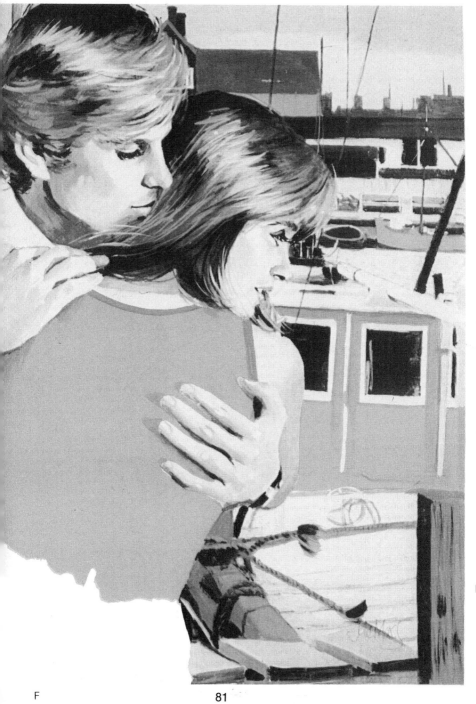

him. They had been constant companions since they met two years before at a friend's eighteenth birthday party.

They had laughed their way through tennis tournaments, knowing they didn't stand a chance of winning, they had raced each other in the local swimming baths and had kissed longingly and lovingly in the moonlight.

Why then had she all these sudden doubts about the future? There was no-one else, and Ross was still the same fun-loving companion.

Silently they walked back to Marie's home. Ross shook his head when she asked him in as usual for coffee.

"No, love, not tonight! I still want you, Marie. Think about it and don't keep me waiting too long for my answer."

Marie felt an unusual warmth behind his good night kiss. Because she knew she had hurt him she held him when he would have let her go.

"A little time, Ross, that's all I need," she whispered.

It was tea-time the next day when Marie's Aunt Hester appeared unexpectedly.

"Sorry to barge in at meal time," she told them, "but I've two hours to wait for my train home and it seemed too good a chance to miss."

Jean Weston hugged her sister.

"Of course it was! You know we always love to see you. Did you have a good holiday?"

"Lovely! Molenbay doesn't seem to change, thank goodness. Afraid I've just been lazy."

That night as she lay in bed Marie thought about Molenbay. A quiet little fishing village, she remembered, as she recalled her holidays there as a child. Gradually she felt a longing for quiet walks on the beach, time to herself — to think . . .

Surprisingly her mother raised no objection.

"It's Ross, love, isn't it?"

"Yes, Mum! I thought I wanted to marry him, but . . ."

"He's a good lad and if he is your choice then Dad and I would be pleased. But it's *your* life, and mistakes are made all too easily. Molenbay should be a good place to relax."

THE head of the typing pool raised no objections when Marie asked for some late holiday time, so Saturday saw her leaving her case at the station and walking along the front looking for somewhere to stay.

She found a small bed and breakfast house overlooking the bay. The shiny brass knocker and spotless muslin curtains boded well, and Marie found herself smiling at the rosy-cheeked woman who answered the door. Soon she was in a small but comfortable room, with a wide window seat, and as she sat drinking the hot tea Mrs Clegg brought her she felt some of her restlessness leave her.

Sunday and Monday were rather cool and Marie went for long walks on the cliffs, and curled up on her window seat, reading.

Tuesday, though, the September sun broke through and Marie stretched out on the rocks, enjoying the warmth.

It was nearly lunchtime when she heard a commotion on the beach. Looking down from her vantage point on the rocks, she saw a group of people watching a man wading from the water with a small child in his arms. Then the group closed round him and he was lost to view.

A few minutes later he appeared just below her. She watched him strip off his wet shirt, but when he began to loosen his shorts she gave an embarrassed cough.

He looked up at her and laughed.

"It's all right," he assured her. "I'm quite respectable! I intended going swimming anyway!"

Marie saw he was wearing swimming trunks under his shorts. He spread his clothes out on the rocks and climbed up beside her.

"Think the birds will enjoy these more than me." He laughed as he opened a wet packet of sandwiches. "At least the chocolate is still OK — I hope! Neil Jeffreys," he added, holding out a hand.

Marie smiled.

"Marie Weston. It was very brave of you to go in the sea like that. It looks so rough."

"Oh, the boy wasn't in deep. Just panicked because he was out of his depth. Someone else would have fished him out if I hadn't."

Marie looked at him shyly, suddenly realising how few young men

▶over

they were first...

WHEN Brian Fletcher rode Red Rum to victory in the 1977 Grand National, the horse completed a historic treble. Red Rum, the nation's favourite "jumper," became the first to win the National three times. It was a fantastic achievement — for apart from the other two wins in 1973 and 1974, the horse finished second in 1975 and 1976!

"Rummy" was retired not long after his final victory and took up a new "career," making many public and TV appearances.

she knew apart from Ross. She liked his quiet smile and rather grave blue eyes. His sandy-coloured hair lay in damp curls and he ran a hand through it trying to restore some sort of order.

"You on holiday?" he asked.

"Mmm, I'm staying in a house on the front. My landlady is a dear — she's packed all these sandwiches. Please, share them."

"If you're sure! The seagulls are making short work of mine." He laughed.

"Do you live round here?"

"No! I'm staying at the convalescent home a couple of miles out. Had a virus and found myself packed off there to recuperate."

They talked easily, finding a joint love of music and autobiography. Neil had a soft, soothing voice and somehow Marie knew instinctively that he could be trusted.

The afternoon flew by and all too soon the sun left them and they walked along the beach to White Cottage. Neil hesitated as she made to leave him.

"Marie," he said slowly, as though unsure of himself. "If you'd like to go for a walk tomorrow I know the area."

"Thanks Neil! I'd love to."

THE weather was kind again and they walked over the moors and ate their picnic lunch in the shelter of a castle ruin. All too soon the day was over and Marie hoped Neil would suggest meeting in the evening. He didn't — but he did suggest cycling round the headland the following day.

"I can borrow two bikes," he assured her. "No problem getting here. I'll ride one and wheel the other. Make me think I'm a boy again."

That night as Marie drifted off to sleep she thought about Neil. He had talked to her about his family back in the South, and in answer to her questions he had told her he was a welfare worker in Symmingdale, about thirty miles away.

She tried to forget that his answers had been slow in coming — how he had hesitated. She remembered his kind, gentle smile, his soft voice, his obvious love of all things beautiful, and couldn't believe he was other than he made out.

Thursday and Friday they spent together. Marie knew she was beginning to care about Neil — but apart from helping her over the rough ground and a gentle touch of his hand when they parted he made no effort to hold her. Once when he helped her zip up her waterproof jacket during a quick shower he looked down at her.

For a moment or two she saw caring in his eyes, almost a strange yearning, but before she could be sure, it had gone and he was laughing because the shower was over before he could wrap up himself.

On the Friday they lingered on the rocks where they had first met.

"Please say something, Neil." Marie found herself whispering to herself. "Don't let it end like this."

Outside White Cottage he took her hands in his.

"Thank you for these last few days, Marie," he said quietly. "I will always remember them."

"Neil!" The word was torn from her and she looked up at him unable to hide her feelings. Then she saw it again. The yearning deep in his eyes and, she was certain, a pain that matched her own.

"Oh, Marie! Be happy, little one."

Swiftly he raised her hands to his lips and then, with his long even stride he walked away, and she knew instinctively that he was walking out of her life.

IN the days that followed her holiday Marie found her thoughts constantly returning to Neil. She remembered the peace, the serenity she had felt with him. She was certain he cared about her.

Was he married? Somehow she felt he would have told her.

Something formed a barrier between them though. If only she could see him again, talk to him.

At least he had made her realise that her feelings for Ross were simply those of a friend. That she could not marry him.

But the thought of not seeing Neil again frightened her. She thought of him constantly.

"Marie, dear, he must be engaged — or even married," her mother told her. "After all, you only knew him for a few days."

"Oh, Mum, there was something about him. I can't explain but I know I have to try to see him again. Can I borrow your car on Sunday? I can't ask for more time off work."

So early on Sunday morning Marie drove down to Symmingdale. It was not a large place, but even so she realised her chances of seeing Neil were very slim. She asked a passer-by where the welfare office was, at least she could look at the place where Neil worked, but the woman looked puzzled.

"We have a small place that opens twice a week, but I don't know of anywhere else."

Marie fought back her tears. Her mother must have been right.

A Time For Giving

CHRISTMAS is a time for giving.
We purchase every gift with care.
Families and friends are gathered ready
For the Christmas fayre.
Homes are filled with joy and laughter,
Now the happy day is here,
Our prayers are filled with true thanksgiving,
Hearts feel humble and sincere
As we count our blessings
Now the busy day is done,
Most of all we thank thee, Father,
For the gift of Thy dear Son.
— Margory Green.

Neil had explained that he was a welfare worker, but . . .

Blindly she turned away from the huddle of buildings and walked up a leafy lane in the direction of the church steeple she could see in the distance. The leaves were falling and Marie scuffed her feet through the gold and russet carpet, remembering how Neil had cupped a leaf in his hand, pointed out its perfect construction. So many lovely things he had shown her.

"Take time, Marie. Time for living. For seeing things about us, simple things anyone can enjoy."

There were a few people making their way into the church, and Marie, the day stretching in front of her, joined them. It was a beautiful church. Early chrysanthemums decorated the altar, and the scent of late roses drifted on the air.

Marie didn't notice the group of brown-clad friars gathered at the back of the church. But one of them noticed Marie . . .

After the service Marie walked away and stood looking over the church wall at the distant countryside. She had tried to find Neil and failed. Pride stopped her making any more enquiries. He knew where she was, but . . .

"Marie!"

The voice came from behind and she turned slowly — unbelievingly.

SHE saw the long brown habit, the hood thrown back from the face she had seen so often in her dreams, and slowly she began to understand.

"I wanted to tell you, but somehow the right words wouldn't come," he told her. "Then I thought it best to let you just forget . . ."

"But you wore other clothes. You were just like an ordinary person!"

"I *am* just an ordinary person." The sweet smile she remembered so well lightened his features. "Look, let's sit on this wall. We have to talk.

"Just because I have chosen a different way of life, it doesn't make me a special person. Our order allows us a certain amount of freedom. We wear our own clothes when off duty and our life is not as austere as that of some of the orders."

Marie listened as he talked of the founder of the order.

"He was just a simple man who didn't seek to be revered. He was of good family but renounced everything for the life he loved. Just as we, his followers, have done.

"I have promised my life to the church, Marie. To helping others and going where I am needed. Perhaps I was wrong to seek your company, but I felt you needed someone. That I could help you by giving you my friendship. If things had been different . . .

"I have thought about you so much, little one. But I know I have to take my chosen path."

He turned to her and saw the tears.

"Please understand," he pleaded. "Please try to understand."

"I do, Neil. But it seems such a waste, when we . . ."

He didn't have to ask her meaning, but he had fought his battle and knew he had made the right decision. He had hoped Marie would accept their parting, but now he was glad she knew. She was young — twenty to his twenty-four — and she would come to terms with life in her own way.

"You know, Marie, that we own nothing of our own. All we need is provided by the order. But I picked up a piece of wood on the beach. I carved it for you, not thinking I would ever be able to give it to you."

He handed her a delicate wood carving of a bird. A seagull in flight.

Marie smiled her thanks, then, in spite of the sun, she shivered. Neil took her hand, drawing her to her feet.

"Come, little one. You're cold."

Somehow they found themselves entering the empty church. Together they knelt. Marie thought she would never see roses or chrysanthemums again without remembering those few minutes in that holy place. Then she felt Neil's hand on her head.

"Bless you, Marie. Be happy."

Marie didn't follow him out of the church. She stood at the door until he was almost lost to sight. He turned and raised a hand in silent farewell. Marie knew she would never see him again.

IT was past lunchtime but Marie had no thought of food as she walked back to the car.

She had thought of all sorts of explanations for Neil's behaviour but not the right one. Somehow it seemed to slot everything into place, and she knew she would always remember him.

Marie looked at the bird still in her hand. It was about three inches in length, every detail perfect. A gift from a man who had nothing, yet still found a way to give.

Slowly the young girl thought about her own life. She knew she could never renounce the world as Neil had done, but perhaps she could do something to help others. She thought about Ross and how they had laughed their way through their time together. She had laughed with Neil, but it had been a different laughter — and their talks had held something deeper than she had found with Ross.

As she sat in the car she felt the hurt she had felt over Neil melt away. A new feeling replaced it. One of gratitude that she had had those few perfect days, that she had learned a deeper insight into life.

Perhaps there would be someone else, one day, but for now she would begin to make something of her life, something she would be proud of.

Carefully she wrapped her handkerchief round the bird, and put it safely away.

Then, without a backward glance she drove away. Back to her home. Her mother would be waiting. □

A LITTLE GIVE And TAKE

by ELSIE JACKSON

I'M off, darling! Back about ten." Ken Robertson popped briefly into the kitchen to kiss his wife on the cheek.

A moment later Tracey heard the front door slam shut behind him. As though it were an echo, a door upstairs banged, too. Then the strains of the latest pop tune came floating downstairs.

Tracey sighed. This was Hazel's favourite method of shutting her out these days.

Suddenly Tracey felt close to tears. She sat down at the kitchen table with her head in her hands. She had had such high hopes this morning.

When she had opened the local paper there had been an advertisement for the old Walt Disney film "Snow White" being shown at the local cinema.

Remembering that this was one of the evenings when Ken taught at the college night school, Tracey had had her brainwave. She would take Hazel to the cinema, then treat her to supper afterwards.

Surely this would thaw out the icy barrier that still existed between herself and her ten-year-old stepdaughter? A barrier that Tracey had been trying in vain to break down for the past six months.

Tracey could hardly wait for Hazel to arrive home from school that afternoon. In fact, she had almost walked down to the school gates.

She was only thankful that she had held back, however, when she saw the curt way in which Hazel rejected her suggestion. Bad enough to receive a brush-off in your own living-room! It would have been highly embarrassing in front of Hazel's friends.

What on earth was she going to do, Tracey wondered miserably. This strained, unhappy situation just could not go on. Ken wasn't

doing anything to help, either. And she hated to make him unhappy by telling him just how weighty the problem had become.

Goodness knows, he had had enough unhappiness in his life, poor darling! She had hoped to make up for that after she married him.

Tracey could still remember the sad, slightly neglected look that Ken had had about him on the evening when she first met him. She had been with the firm for a month, working as Mr Argyll's private secretary, when she had been invited to one of the frequent cheese-and-wine parties the Argylls had at home.

In actual fact, she had already bought a ticket for a performance of the "Barber Of Seville," a one-night production by a famous national touring company. But unwilling to offend her boss, she had reluctantly returned the ticket to the box office. She had been standing with Mrs Argyll by the fireplace when Ken had walked through the door.

"Now that's Ken Robertson, the firm's chief accountant," Mrs Argyll had whispered. "Brilliant young man. Only thirty. But what a tragic life he's had, poor lad. His wife died of some rare virus six years ago.

"He's got a little girl of eight," Mrs Argyll had added. "But she lives with her grandparents in Westcot. Ken lives on his own in a service flat. Come on over, and I'll introduce you."

TRACEY and Ken had only had time to exchange a murmured greeting, when the Argylls' son switched on the hi-fi and people had to shout to make their voices heard above the noise of the music.

Neither Tracey nor Ken made the effort, but stood together in silence until the record came to an end.

"And I might have been listening to Rossini," Tracey murmured, without thinking.

Then realising how ungrateful and superior she must sound, she blushed bright red.

But Ken's grey eyes had lit up with interest and amusement.

"Do you know," he said in a low voice, "I was thinking exactly the same thing myself. Are you an opera fan?"

Then, without quite knowing how it happened, Tracey found that she had told this pale, handsome young man her life story.

About growing up on a farm miles from anywhere. And suddenly discovering the joys of concert halls and theatres when she moved to the city to take a business course at college. About how her parents had moved to Australia, but she had decided to stay on in Scotland.

Finally she told him how the city firm she had been working for had gone into liquidation, so she had come to Glengarnock to work in McDonald's Brewery.

"And do you like it here?" Ken had asked.

"I think so," Tracey had told him. "I'm just finding my way around."

"There's a very good Concert Club," Ken had told her. "I'm a member. Perhaps you would like to come with me one evening?"

Of course, she had said "yes." For already they had both realised that something rather special had happened to them in the past ten minutes.

In a matter of weeks Tracey knew she couldn't live happily without this quiet, gentle, humorous man. She had written to tell her mother so.

What about the little girl? Tracey's mother had written back. *Might you not have difficulties there, love? I can't help thinking it's an awful lot for you to take on at your age.*

Mum, Tracey had replied in amused exasperation. *I am twenty-four, you know. And I've always been good with youngsters. Don't you remember how I loved helping with the Sunday school and the Brownies?*

Besides, young Hazel's been living with her grandparents. So it's not as though I'm depriving her of her dad's company.

Anyway, we're not going to rush the marriage. We want to have a bungalow built and have everything ready for Hazel to come to us.

What Tracey hadn't told her parents was Ken's admission that Hazel had been very spoiled by his in-laws.

Presenting Christmas!

NO wealth attended at His birth,
　Yet riches did He bring,
Reflected through inspiring words
　The choral voices sing.

No costly jewels of His own,
　But in the midnight sky,
The massed array of stars shone forth
　As diamond drops on high.

The crystal moon left silver glow,
　And mist its pearly sheen.
And stars, an ivory shining light
　To guild this hallowed scene.

But more than this, the love He brought —
　Eternal love from birth,
Continues to enrich the joys
　That we may share on earth . . .
　　　— *Elizabeth Gozney.*

"I don't mean that she's rude or unpleasant," he had explained. "But they've just let her do what she wants. She's never done well at school, not because she's not bright, but because she's lazy.

"Gran and Grandpa never worried her about her lessons, you see," he'd added. "If she was happy, that was all that mattered to them."

And I'm afraid that's all that will matter to me, to begin with, Tracey had thought secretly. She hadn't been too worried by Hazel's reserve in the initial stages of getting to know the little girl.

It was only natural, after all, that the child should be a little wary of this stranger who was about to play such an important part in her life.

KEN'S mother-in-law, a plump, gentle woman, had been encouraging.

"She'll come round, dearie," she had told Tracey. "She couldn't have got a nicer stepmother. I've told her that . . . her mum would have been happy about it, too," she added shyly.

Tracey hugged her for that.

But despite everyone's good wishes Tracey had not made her breakthrough. Hazel had come to Glengarnock, had started her new school without any undue fuss, had quickly made friends, but had kept up her attitude of frigid reserve towards Tracey.

What Tracey feared, above everything else, was the effect this might eventually have on Ken and herself. Ken had been so confident in her ability to win Hazel round.

"That won't be any problem," he had stated firmly. "What worries me is the thought of changing the lazy little monkey into a hard-working schoolgirl. She'll soon be moving on to secondary school. She'll have to pull her socks up."

Oh, Ken! If she would only smile at me! I wouldn't care if she was bottom of the class, she had felt like yelling. But of course she hadn't.

★   ★   ★   ★

Tracey looked at the clock. Quarter to seven! This would never do. She was frittering away the evening. Tracey had given up her job after her marriage, and she still felt guilty at the amount of leisure time she now seemed to have.

Ken would tease her about it.

"I don't feel as if I've *earned* a free evening," she would tell him. "I can't just sit about without doing anything."

This was why Ken had bought her the sewing machine. And as she thought of the gleaming, new electric machine sitting in the hall cupboard in its plastic overcoat, Tracey's face clouded. She supposed she had better battle with the fiendish contraption again.

Ken had asked again this evening how the new living-room curtains were coming on.

She could not bring herself to tell him that the material was still in its wrapping paper, untouched.

"But anyone can use a sewing machine." He had laughed when Tracey had protested that sewing and knitting had never been her forte . . . "And anyone can make curtains. Especially a super-efficient secretary like you."

Tracey brought the machine in and set it down on the table, letting the foot control drop gently on to the floor. She had made several attempts to sew a straight line on old scraps of material, none of them with any success.

Now she unwrapped the blue-and-silver brocade curtain material and frowned at it. Ken was right. This was absurd. She ought to be able to make curtains, for goodness' sake.

She quickly tacked along the foot of one length of material, read through the machine's instruction book again, and raised the little metal footplate.

Then almost instantly she let out a howl of despair. Her line of sewing had veered off wildly, right across the width of the material.

It was the last straw. Tracey pounded her fist again and again on the kitchen table, then laid her head on her arms and began to cry.

Suddenly she felt her shoulder being shaken. She looked up to find Hazel's grey eyes regarding her with amazement.

WHAT'S wrong?" the girl asked. "Aren't you well?"

Tracey was too upset to think about her pride, or worry about how she must appear to the child.

"It's that stupid machine!" She sobbed. "Look what it's done now! Ruined that lovely material! And it was so expensive, too. I don't know what your father's going to say."

Hazel looked positively astounded at this. Then suddenly she sat down on the edge of the table. She gently freed the curtain material from the machine, and took it on her knee.

"It's not ruined at all," she said quietly. "Look. All you need to do is snip the stitches out."

She did this. Then with an uncertain glance at Tracey she asked, "Can I look at the machine?"

Tracey nodded, sniffing loudly.

▶over

they were first...

THE Sixties was the decade of space exploration — and it was very much a man's world. So, it isn't hard to imagine the shock waves Valentina Tereshkova sent right round the globe.

On June 16, 1963, this Russian cosmonaut became the first woman to orbit the earth in a space-flight that was eventually to last almost three days. She returned to Earth safely — and the whole world joined to share the triumph of her historic achievement.

"Well! No wonder!" Hazel exclaimed after a moment. "You had the tension wrong. And the footplate wasn't down."

"I'm sorry," Tracey said humbly, then suddenly she began to giggle.

"That was what I was always saying in the sewing class at school," she added. "Once we had an inspector round. And she lifted up my cream pullover I was trying to knit, and said, 'A very nice dishcloth, my dear. Carry on!' "

Hazel threw back her head and let out a long, rippling laugh.

"Shall I do the curtains for you, then?" she asked.

"Can you?" asked Tracey in awe.

"Of course," Hazel said indignantly. "I sewed lots of things for Gran. I love sewing."

Tracey stood up and Hazel took over her place at the machine. Some time later a perfectly-finished curtain lay on the table.

Tracey's admiration was quite unfeigned.

"Hazel!" she exclaimed. "That's absolutely wonderful! You're so clever! I suppose that's what your dad thought I should be able to do. He wouldn't listen when I said I couldn't."

"I know," Hazel said suddenly. "I think it's because he can do everything, I think. He doesn't understand that I find my lessons hard. Especially my English. He thinks I'm just lazy."

Tracey looked at the small, solemn-faced girl with a new understanding.

"Do you know what, Hazel?" she said. "We could help each other. English was always my best subject at school. Supposing you gave me sewing lessons, and I helped you with *your* lessons?"

Oh, don't let her go behind her barrier again, Tracey was praying silently as Hazel considered this proposition. But there was no need to worry.

"Yes. All right," Hazel said finally, and for the first time since Tracey had met her she gave her a warm, wide smile.

"I thought you were like Dad, too," the girl added suddenly. "I mean terribly clever. Able to do everything."

"Not a bit of it," Tracey said quietly.

Dare I suggest it, she was wondering. Or would I be pushing my luck? But before she could speak, Hazel said shyly:

"I don't suppose we could go to the second house of 'Snow White'?"

"And not get home until eleven?" Tracey asked in a shocked tone. Then as the little girl's face dropped, she added gaily, "Why not? Just for once. If we hurry we'll have time for an ice-cream before we go in. We'll leave your dad a note."

"Gosh! I wonder what he'll say." Hazel giggled conspiratorially.

"Who cares?" Tracey said, giving her a wink. "We're two against one."

But that's not quite right, she thought, as she and Hazel hurried down the road to the bus stop.

We're three now. Together. And her heart sang for happiness. □

Wild Poppies

THOUGH the poets sing your praises,
    Farmers look on you with scorn,
When you thread your scarlet ribbons
    Through their fields of ripening corn.
Little poppies, silken poppies,
    Pert and pretty as you please,
Like tiny Romanies you greet us,
    Red skirts, fluttering in the breeze.

Black-eyed poppies, ever cheerful,
    Bright as paint, and full of fun,
How it lifts the heart to see you,
    Dancing gaily in the sun!
Though you cannot vie in beauty
    With your sisters, it is true,
No other flower can hold a candle
    To the brilliance of your hue.

Evocative of deeds of glory,
    In a darker, bygone year,
Though bitter-sweet the thoughts you
      kindle,
    One and all we hold you dear.
And many a tired old face will soften,
    Remembering some well-loved name,
At the sight of one wild poppy,
    Glowing, steadfast as a flame.
          — *Kathleen O'Farrell.*

Keeping It In The Family

by KATE CLAYTON

THE frozen tank was the last straw! Not only was the cottage comfortless and cold, but an alarming trickle of water was making its way down the stairs, darkening the delicate rose-pink carpet which we had cherished for years.

"The tank's burst!" Tim exclaimed. "Not that I'm surprised, considering the weather outside."

"What shall I do?" I wailed.

"Find a plumber," he said. "Sharpish."

"They'll all be up to their necks," I said, "and we're not even locals, not really."

"Pearson's have done work for us in the past. Come on, let's try them. Why the deuce didn't we have a phone installed when we bought this place?"

"You said . . ." I began. "You said we wanted peace and quiet and —" But he interrupted.

"Come on!"

We climbed back into the car. It had been a long cold journey, and although we had stopped for lunch in Dorchester we were both tired and hungry, and had been looking forward to sitting down in our little chintzy dining-room and consuming the Cumberland pie I had brought with me.

Luckily, Pearson's were sympathetic to our
plight and despatched one of their workmen right away.

"It's been down to minus twelve here these past few days," he
remarked in his rich Dorset accent, as he surveyed our small but
depressing disaster. "You be lucky . . ."

He then went off into a lengthy description of unspeakable horrors
in surrounding properties, and finally managed to procure for us a
supply of cold water only, which meant we could, at least, use the loo.

"Can't get a new tank until Monday morning," he muttered.
"Everyone will be closed up for the weekend, see."

We expressed our gratitude in an acceptable manner and he went
off in the direction of the pub.

G

"I'll bet you slipped him too much," I said, knowing Tim's tendency to over-tip, but he was too busy switching on everything which would switch on to bother with a reply.

"Thank heavens the cooker works," he remarked. "Let's get on with the supper. I'm starving."

I went to bed that night wearing two pullovers over my nightie and Tim's golf socks. The under-blankets had done their stuff but beds cool with remarkable swiftness when temperatures are minus twelve outside, and the following morning as we huddled over breakfast, he said:

"You know, Jeannie, we're getting too old for this sort of caper. I've a feeling the time might have come to sell the cottage."

"Sell Holly Cottage!" I gasped. "But we've had it for nearly twenty years. Where would we go the first two weeks in May to enjoy the blossom? And what would the children do?"

"The children, dear heart, are all grown up," Tim said. "Catherine and Peter are settled in their comfortable police house. Rob and Pat have their little town house and Mark his flat over his estate agency."

"But they all use the cottage," I insisted. "They *love* it — just as much as we do."

Tim didn't reply. He seemed to be immersed in the removal of the top of his boiled egg.

I TOOK a quick swallow of tea, and then went on.

"I can't visualise life without Holly Cottage." My gaze wandered round the rose-white walls, the poppies-in-the-corn curtains, the old warming pan, and the map of Hardy's Wessex which Peter had discovered in Maisie's little antique shop in the middle of the High Street.

Tim still didn't reply.

"D'you remember," I said, "when we were uncertain whether we should buy the place? The surveyor had warned us about the roof. He practically predicted its imminent collapse!"

Tim's face relaxed then. He even smiled.

"And it's stood for seventeen years, and borne the weight of a brand-new thatch! These old cob cottages that have survived for over two hundred years refuse to comply with surveyors' reports."

I began stacking plates and dishes — the original Cottage Rose design which were still more or less intact minus a few chips. My mind was whirling because of Tim's remark and I had to keep on talking.

"D'you remember," I gabbled on, "the time Peter brought his two puppies here and they got the idea it was *their* territory and wouldn't allow poor old Jasper over his own doorstep?"

"Those were the days," Tim agreed, and he sighed and looked suddenly, not old, but older. "But it's the future we have to consider now, Jeannie. It's hard work keeping two homes going, and you know, I've felt guilty about it more than once."

"But you let people come," I protested. "What about old Mrs

Jackson, and the minister, and Dr Anderson? They all recuperated here, and many others beside. We've never been selfish about the place, and it's never made us any money."

"But it could now," said Tim. "It will have increased in value over the years, and I'm thinking the time has come to cash in."

He frowned. "Let's get Mark to value the place in the spring, and take it from there?"

"Why wait till spring?" I mumbled angrily. "Why not next week?"

"The daffodils will be blooming then, and you know how pretty the old orchard looks. The bluebells will be showing in the wood, too. We've got to be practical, Jeannie."

Suddenly his wide, warm smile flashed out and I felt my bad temper melting away.

"Now," he said, "let's concentrate on our personal celebration. I suppose you realise it's only a few weeks to our ruby wedding? How about popping off to Tahiti on the proceeds of the cottage sale?"

I grimaced. "You know very well, Tim Warbrick, I hate flying, and boiling hot beaches bring me out in blisters."

Tim pretended to recoil at this flood of alliteration, and I had to laugh.

"OK," I said, "let me think about it. You've sprung this on me all of a sudden, and all because of a frozen tank!"

"No, love." His smile was strained now. "It's been in my mind for several months. I'm not as young as I was, and I'll always be quite a bit older than you."

"You're all right though?" I asked quickly. "What did Dr Anderson say when you had that check-up? You were very cagey when you came home. You never will talk about yourself."

"He said I was fine." Tim grinned. "Just needing to lose a bit of weight, and ease up a bit . . ."

He looked uncomfortable and guilty and I felt a flood of remorse.

"Oh, darling, I'm being selfish!" I told him. "Of course, you're right. It's time we sold the cottage, and as you say we can go places on the extra money."

THERE was consternation in the family when we broke the news about the cottage!

"But you *can't*!" Rob cried. "It's part of the family. It's a retreat . . . a bolt-hole . . . a sanctuary, a security, too."

"The children will be heartbroken," Pat put in.

But Mark said, "It's hard work and responsibility for Mum and Dad. Something they could well do without now."

He stuck his chest out in an exaggerated gesture. "Leave it to me. The boss is always on the lookout for sound, cared-for country cottages, and I'll get him to let me handle this one personally.

"Tell you what, though; why don't we have a last family reunion there? We'll call it a spit-and-polish party and finish off all the outstanding jobs. And make a memory, too."

I had to stifle a flood of tears at his last sentence. Making a memory seemed so horribly final.

But leaving it all to our capable son was a load off Tim's shoulders, and on the day we set off on the last project, I had come to terms with the situation.

We didn't tell the children the exact object of the exercise, and Paul, aged nine, wanted to know what a spit-and-polish party meant.

"It means," supplied his slightly older sister, Clare, "a clean-up. Something you need, right now."

It was a squash, piling eight of us into a three-bedroomed cottage, but the children were thrilled to bed down in the summer-house, and with the aid of a couple of folding beds we were able to manage it.

With so many willing hands, results began to show almost immediately. The blue walls in the big bedroom rapidly acquired the azure of summer skies with the application of a single coat of quick-drying emulsion paint.

Ceilings which had been slowly yellowing, became whiter than white, and window-sills glowed red and old oak black.

Lights Of Home

THE lights of home, through a hazy mist,
  Beckon me awhile,
And yielding to my fancies flight,
I walk my heather isle,
To where the shimmering waterfall
Cascades the burblin' burn,
The pool, where weans guddled trout,
Till homeward, weary steps we'd turn,
At that magic hour twixt light and gloam,
When shadows flee and the lights of home,
Would beckon me.
        — *Katherine MacIntyre.*

In the garden, the children, directed by Mark, planted wallflowers and pansies in profusion, and helped carry to the growing bonfire enormous prunings of lilac, forsythia and weeping ash.

In the middle of it all Maisie appeared with an antique spinning wheel which she thought we might like to have standing in front of the old bread oven beside the hearth. On hearing the news her face fell.

"We'll miss you for sure, Mr and Mrs Warbrick," she mourned. "You seem as much part of the village as any of us. I do hope you'll be able to sell to folk who'll fit in."

She took the spinning wheel away sadly, and Mark helped her load it into her van.

"I feel awful about it," I told him later. "She's been searching for that for years. We'd practically promised to buy it." I gave him a speculative glance. "How would you like to buy it for us for a ruby wedding present?"

"We've already got your present," Mark said, and grinned mischievously.

Keeping It In The Family

THE day we left Holly Cottage was one of those perfect spring days which are always so unexpected. The holly tree was actually in blossom, and Rob, who was good at botany, said: "There'll be lots of berries for Christmas. We must remember to cover up one or two boughs with netting, or the redwings might get them all again."

Nobody had the heart to comment on this, although looks passed.

On the morning of our fortieth wedding anniversary, Peter — being our eldest son — dropped the bomb. We were all assembled in our living-room at home. There were flowers and messages everywhere, and a quite delightful cake, baked and decorated by Catherine, stood immersed in ruby-red ribbons in the centre of the table.

Tim and I couldn't believe what he was trying to tell us. How could they possibly afford to *buy* Holly Cottage — even with five of them clubbing together? It just didn't make sense.

"It's a business proposition," Mark explained, taking over from Peter. "We've formed a company and we shall run the cottage in a business-like manner. No more free holidays for deserving cases, not at present anyway, and no personal perks until it's making a profit."

"How come?" Tim demanded a bit dangerously.

"By personalised lettings," Peter said. "To friends, friends of friends and other distinguished clientèle. We've worked it all out and are sure it can be done. We'll share the maintainence between us.

"I shall keep the accounts, Robert will supervise renovations and repairs, and Mark will do the actual letting through his office."

"We'll let for all the summer months, and do the maintainance in winter," Mark added. "Apart from the first two weeks in May each year. These will be permanently reserved!"

"Those were *our* two weeks," I murmured.

"Exactly!" chorused the whole family, and then they were all clapping their hands and laughing.

"Two weeks every May is your ruby wedding present. And if anything goes wrong — even a frozen tank — all you have to do is to contact Warbrick Trust!"

We stood there, the two of us, in the warm loving circle of our family, and tried to take it all in.

The two children advanced then, giggling fit to kill. Between them they were carrying a scroll tied with ruby-red ribbons.

"It's a contract," they managed to splutter, "for you to sign."

When they'd all gone home, after a round of hugs, kisses, explanations and legal details, I had a little weep.

"What have we done to deserve it?"

"Nothing," Tim said.

"Nothing comes from nothing." I sniffed, blowing my nose.

"You make it sound like an operetta!" Tim hated emotional scenes.

"It is!" I cried, recalling from my subconscious an old family favourite incorporating music, mountains and melodrama.

It had a happy ending, too! □

One Christmas To Remember

HEATHER GRANT stood by the bedroom window. Cold December rain battered on the pane, blurring the view of black rocks and swaying trees. Stupid as it may seem, this was not what she had expected.

Heather's memories had been so full of sunshine and long summer holidays spent here in this house, that this winter bleakness had taken her by surprise.

"Any sign of the ambulance yet?" Her aunt's unsteady voice came from the bed behind her.

"No. Not yet, Aunt Liz," said Heather.

Liz Munro was Heather's mother's aunt. And Dhucrag had been the house where Heather's mother had grown up.

by JENNIE BOLWELL

In those days the house had stood in the midst of a thriving farm, and Heather's grandfather and her uncles had worked the surrounding fields. But after the war the land had had to be sold off and eventually only Aunt Liz had been left living in the old house. But even during Heather's childhood, Dhucrag had been a wonderful place to spend summer holidays.

Aunt Liz had organised the days for her nieces and nephews and yes, her great-nieces and great-nephews, too, so their holidays would be full of excitement — mountain climbing, and fishing trips, picnics and fun.

102

"Can I get you anything, Aunt Liz? Are you in pain?" Heather asked, turning from the window.

"Och, the pain isn't too bad, lass," Aunt Liz said. "I am just a wee bit worried — that's all." Her eyes were shut.

"Please don't worry," Heather said. "I'll come with you in the ambulance."

The old woman looked up in alarm.

"No, no! I am not worried about that. No! Don't come with me. There isn't a bus back till very late. No, no! I'll be as right as rain in the hospital."

It was only a day or two ago, in a bustling London suburb, that Heather had arrived home from technical college to find her mother reading a letter. Her face looked stricken.

"What is wrong, Mum?" she had asked.

"It's Aunt Liz. Sounds as if she is ill! This letter's from a neighbour who lives a good mile from Dhucrag. She says that Aunt Liz is becoming very frail, but hasn't been to see a doctor. She even suspects that the old lady might be in pain!"

Aunt Liz — frail? Spry, energetic Aunt Liz — an old lady? Heather just could not imagine it.

"I shall have to go to her," Heather's mother had said. "I'll ask the boss for some time off and get up there to Argyllshire."

"No, Mum! Please let me go. Probably all she needs is someone to look after her for a while," Heather had said. "You know that this course I am doing at college isn't what I really want, anyway. So please let me drop it and go to Dhucrag."

So it had been arranged and Heather had set off on the long journey north. But she had found things worse than she had expected when she'd arrived. She had called Dr Harrison right away and he had scolded Aunt Liz for not summoning him sooner. He had also insisted that she go to the hospital in Oban for further tests.

YOU mustn't worry about the house, Aunt Liz," Heather said now, smiling at the old woman. "I will have it looking like a new pin for you coming back to."

"Och, lass! I'm not bothered about the house. It will be here long after I have gone!" Liz Munro said wryly. "But you will look after Skip, won't you?"

At the sound of his name, the old dog thumped his tail. He was lying on the rug by the bed. "He is lazy about walks now, but he does need a pat now and then."

"Yes, yes! Of course!"

"Sophie will be no bother," Liz Munro went on. "There is plenty of tinned catmeat in the cupboard, but when the fishman calls on a Tuesday, I usually buy her some cod scraps."

"I'll do that, Aunt Liz."

"And the hens! Remember to collect the eggs."

"I will remember."

Suddenly Aunt Liz gave a chuckle.

104

"Heather!" she said. "Do you remember, dear, how you used to have to chase after Ginger and Bing when they escaped out of their field?"

Oh yes! Heather remembered all right. They had been young donkeys then — and such rascals! Many a hot summer's day she had raced after them with her pockets bulging with carrots and a rope to lasso them.

"They don't behave like that now, do they?" Heather asked somewhat apprehensively.

Aunt Liz shook her head.

"They have learned with old age. They are happy enough to go in and out of the barn and have the freedom of their own field. As long as you feed them twice a day and see they have plenty of warm hay round their ankles in this cold weather, they should be fine. But, Heather!"

"Yes?"

"Talk to them sometimes — and tell them . . ."

"What shall I tell them?"

"That . . . Oh, tell them — I'll be back!"

Heather ran to the bed and put her arms round her aunt.

"Oh, yes! Yes! I will!" she said.

"And, Heather!"

The old lady's voice was wavery. "If it snows . . ."

". . . I will close the barn door," Heather finished. "I promise, Aunt Liz! I won't let them catch a chill!"

Liz Munro gave a deep sigh.

"Thank you, Heather! I am grateful to you for coming all this way. I feel I can go into hospital now with an easy mind."

Heather went back to the window. But minutes later Aunt Liz spoke again.

"I am sorry now that I didn't have the phone put in. I never felt the need for it till now. It would have been handy for you. When I get to the hospital, I will try to get word to Noel Mitchelson. He could look in on you occasionally and see that everything is all right with you here."

▶p108

LOTS of visitors' first impression of the Isle of Skye, overleaf, is Kyleakin. It's here in this charming village that the ferry from Kyle of Lochalsh lands. It's a place steeped in history, much of which surrounds the ruins of Castle Moil. They overlook the pier, and it's said that the daughter of the Norse king who built the castle had a chain stretched across the strait and charged each ship that passed a toll. The Viking connection is strong, as it's more than likely Kyleakin was named after King Haakon of Norway who sailed past on his way to the Battle of Largs in 1263.

KYLEAKIN, Isle Of Skye : J CAMPBELL KERR

Noel Mitchelson? Yes, Heather remembered him. He was one of the boys who used to come to play with her and her cousins. He liked to take charge. He always knew more than she did, she remembered, and used to tell her what to do.

"He is a vet now," Liz Munro said. "He lives with his parents on the other side of the hill from here. It is a mile or two by road, but —"

"No! Please don't worry about me, Aunt Liz. I would much rather cope on my own. Honestly!"

Heather now saw the headlights of a vehicle turn off the main road and on to the farm track.

"I think that's the ambulance now," she said. "Yes. It is coming past the farm cottages now and is headed towards the house."

Her aunt Liz pushed back the quilt. "Direct them into the back yard to the door. Would you please, dear?"

"Yes. I will. But take your time. I'll come back and help you down the stairs."

Heather went down to meet the ambulance men. They hadn't needed any directions. Liz Munro had never used the front door after she had taken on the house on her own.

She had always maintained that the house was warmer when the big storm doors were bolted against the prevailing winds. And anyhow the hub of the house had always been the big farm kitchen. All the local people knew this.

It wasn't until the ambulance was on its way back down the track that the loneliness of the empty house began to have its effect on Heather.

"Come on, Skip!" she said to the old dog, who was cocking one ear at her, as though he was puzzled. "Let's go and talk to the donkeys."

NEXT day, Andrew the postman thumped on the back door, opened it as he always did, and put the mail on the kitchen table.

In spite of what her aunt had said about not bothering about the house, Heather was determined to have it aired and comfortable for her coming home, so she was busy cleaning the front sitting-room when she heard him. She ran to speak to him.

"Will you take my letter with you, Andrew, please?" she asked.

She had written a big long letter to her parents explaining all that had happened. She tried to hide her loneliness, but she begged them to write soon.

"Sure! I'll take it," Andrew said and went off in his red van.

A day or two later, Heather was in the donkey field with their halters intending to take them for a walk as she used to do. Suddenly Bing threw up his head and gave a very loud hee-haw, and then another.

A car had just driven up the track and a young man got out and came towards the field.

"Sorry!" he said. "Bing knows me and always greets me like that. I am Noel Mitchelson. Here, let me help you. Donkeys can be awkward at times!"

Heather waved a carrot under Bing's nose and managed to get the halter on, then she turned round. Noel had grown taller and his shoulders were broader, but the thick dark hair and the teasing eyes were the same.

"No, thanks. I'll manage," she said.

"I came to ask you if you would like a lift to Oban to visit your aunt, this evening," he said.

"Oh, yes, please!" Heather said. "That's very kind of you."

"Then I will help you walk the donkeys now," he said, and jumping the gate, he put Ginger's halter on without trouble.

"Don't be too worried if your aunt seems a bit drowsy," Noel said as they walked. "I believe she was having some tests done today."

Heather tried not to worry, but later the sight of her aunt lying listless and pale in her hospital bed frightened her.

★　　　★　　　★　　　★

The ward itself was bright and cheery and festooned with Christmas garlands. On the cabinet by Aunt Liz's bed there were Christmas cards among the get well cards. No mail had come to the house. Heather had looked specially.

She had been hoping for a letter or even a card for herself. But everyone seemed to have forgotten her — even her parents.

"The animals?" Aunt Liz whispered.

"All fine!" Heather said, gripping her aunt's hand.

"And you?" Aunt Liz whispered again.

"Me, too, Aunt Liz!" Heather managed to smile very brightly.

Noel Mitchelson gave Liz Munro all the local news, then it was time to leave. On the way home to Dhucrag, Noel looked across at Heather.

"Can I come in for a coffee?" he asked.

"Oh yes. Please do," she said. And she was very glad of his company going into the big dark house. She made coffee and Noel raked at the stove until the peats blazed up and warmed the kitchen.

"What are you going to do with yourself on Christmas Day?" he asked as they sat opposite each other in the large kitchen. "Have you made any plans?"

"Good heavens! I have been so worried I hadn't given it a thought!" Heather said, sipping her mug of coffee. But thinking about it now, she rather dreaded it — all on her own.

"Then why not come and spend it with my parents and me? You and I will be the youngest there, I am afraid. The rest are older relations."

She put down her coffee. Somehow that sounded very nice. "You and I," he had said. Her heart lifted.

"Thank you very much. I'll look forward to that," she said.

HOWEVER, on the morning of Christmas Eve she awoke to a shock! The world was white with snow. Her first thought was for the animals.

Quickly she dressed and dashed downstairs. Old Skip was all right, lying warm on the kitchen rug. But what happened to a cat in the snow?

Heather opened the back door and dashed over to the donkey field. Both donkeys were sheltering in the barn. And curled up in the hay was Sophie, the cat.

"Sorry, my pets!" she said. "I'll soon have you dry and warm."

She brushed the donkeys down, talking to them all the while, then she fed them and raked the hay round their ankles. Then she shut the barn door to keep out the blizzard.

Next she collected the eggs and attended to the hens. First thing she did when she got back to the house was check the kitchen table for mail. But there was still nothing!

Outside the snow was piling, deepening all the while. Then the truth suddenly dawned on her. She was snowed in! Nothing would get in. And she would not be able to get out!

All day it snowed. Dhucrag became imprisoned in a great white blanket. As the afternoon wore on, sheer loneliness drove her back out to see the animals in the barn. Skip went at her heels. All her fears were at their worst.

She remembered her aunt's words — "Tell them I will be back." But her eyes filled with tears, and all she could see in her mind's eye was the pale face of her sick aunt. She put her arms round Ginger's neck — for her own comfort — and prayed silently.

Suddenly Bing pawed the ground with his hooves and let out a loud "hee-haw" followed by another and another. Skip began to bark. Alarmed, Heather looked towards the barn door. It was shaking as though someone was trying to open it. Impossible!

Then suddenly it did open and a huge snowman stepped inside. He shook himself. Noel! On skis!

"Sorry if I frightened you," he said, "but I have brought some good news! The only way to reach you was to come over the hill. I

▶*p112*

FOUNDED in 1136 by David I, Melrose Abbey has certainly been in the wars throughout its history. Repeatedly sacked, it finally fell into ruin around the middle of the 16th century. It must have been a beautiful building — for even what stands today is impressive. Melrose itself is a popular tourist town and home of a well-known seven-a-side rugby tournament. Many visitors come especially to see Abbotsford, the home of Sir Walter Scott, which lies nearby. The lovely Borders countryside around the town was a constant source of inspiration for his novels.

MELROSE ABBEY, Borders : J CAMPBELL KERR

called in at the hospital this morning and the results of the tests have been good. Your aunt will probably need to take medication — for the rest of her life — but the doctor assures me that it can be a long one — as long as she takes reasonable care of herself."

"Oh! That is wonderful!" Heather said. "Thank you!" The tears in her eyes were happy ones now. "Can I offer you some hot coffee?"

"The hotter the better!" he said, propping his skis at the door.

"Can you ski?" he asked her as he followed her across the snowy yard to the back door.

"No! Why?"

"Because our farm is as cut off as Dhucrag, and since I am the only vet on duty tomorrow for miles around, I'll have to stay near a phone."

"Oh dear! Never mind! At least I'll have the animals for company!" she said.

She was heartened by the concern she saw in his eyes. But tomorrow — Christmas Day — was going to be bleak.

Winter Deep . . .

RUFFLED pigeons roost in the eaves,
Frosted snow coats trees and leaves.
Winter blankets hedge and field,
Doors shut tight and windows sealed.

Footmarks in the snow will lead
To where the deer and rabbits feed.
Fronds of ice on every bough,
Winter has a firm grip now.

Birds grow hungry, robins fight,
Woods glow golden, in balmy light.
Against the sky the trees stand bare
Casting strange dark shadows there.

The new moon glistens on the snow,
A woodcock passes to and fro.
The eve is soundless, chilled by frost
And pigeons, warm, in sleep are lost.

The night is sharp, the moonlight clear,
Silhouettes of the hills appear,
Nothing stirs amidst the cold,
A night lies in winter's hold.
— *Polly Pullar.*

It was while they were having their second cup of coffee that a strange loud rumbling noise was heard outside.

"What on earth can that be?" Heather asked, as she went to the front window to look out. The snow had stopped and the moon was bright.

"Sounds like a snow plough or a gritter," Noel said. "But it can't be. They never come off the main road."

"It's getting closer," Heather told him.

He followed her to the window.

"It certainly looks like a gritter," Heather said. "And it's stopped outside the farm cottages."

Noel laughed. "That explains it," he said. "Hugh Logan drives the gritter and his girlfriend lives there. But I had better be off," he said, looking at his watch. "Sure you will be all right?"

"Yes. Of course! And thank you — for your company, and for bringing me the good news."

She had just watched him disappear into the night when she heard an even stranger sound. It was a bell — ringing! But there was no phone! Skip barked.

"What is it, Skip?" she asked the old dog.

He got up from his rug and went to the front door. The bell rang again. Heather opened the inner glass door to reach the big storm door, and tripped over something. It was a bundle of mail! There must have been a new postman on over Christmas!

"I am coming!" she shouted, stepping over the welcome bundle.

She tugged hard at the heavy bolt and at last it slid across with a shriek. The door opened and there on the step stood two snow-covered figures.

M UM! Dad!" Heather couldn't believe her eyes!
"Didn't you get our letter?" her mother said as she stepped inside.

"Oh, come in! Come in! This is so wonderful!" Heather said as she hugged her father and dragged him through to the warmth of the kitchen.

There round the stove, with hot drinks in their hands, Heather learned how they had got here.

"We made our arrangements early on," her mother said, "to spend Christmas at Dhucrag and see for ourselves how things were with Aunt Liz. But we just couldn't understand why you didn't reply to our letter."

"The snow isn't nearly so bad further south," her father put in. "So we reached Oban without much trouble, by train. But of course, we discovered when we got there that no taxi would attempt to bring us out this way in the snow."

"Then how did you manage it?" Heather asked in amazement.

"Well! We were in a small hotel in Oban," her mother said, "intending to stay for the night, when your father got talking to a young chap in the bar —"

"It turned out that he drives the road gritter," her father broke in. "And he was —"

"Hugh!" Heather laughed. "Coming to see his girlfriend!"

"Yes!" They all laughed.

The hands of the clock were approaching midnight.

"Merry Christmas!" they said to one another.

"One last thing I must do!" said Heather with a chuckle. "I'll explain later but I must let the donkeys know that Aunt Liz will definitely be coming home!" □

by ELSPETH RAE

114

WHAT AN INTRODUCTION!

IF anyone had asked Robert Parker what he first saw in Jenny Blair, he would have said she possessed an air of perfect tranquillity.

Then he might have gone on to explain that, at around eleven o'clock on any weekday morning, the foreign exchange department of the bank where he worked was a scene of frantic activity. But that if you wandered into the manager's office you would find a little island of calm.

At its centre would be Jenny Blair, her glossy auburn head bent over her typewriter. Somehow, as soon as you spoke to Jenny, who was the manager's secretary, you felt soothed. The grey eyes she raised to you were always untroubled — no matter what the crisis — and often had a twinkle of humour in them. And her voice was never raised.

A musical voice it was, too, with its lilting West-Coast accent. No wonder Mr Smith, the manager, thought the world of her! She had come to him straight from commercial college and had been with him for three years now.

When Robert had diffidently mentioned one lunchtime to a few of his colleagues that he was going to ask Jenny out in the near future, their response was not encouraging.

Jenny was a very reserved girl, they told him. She had never gone out with anyone in the bank, even though some had asked her several times. It was rumoured that she had a steady boyfriend hidden away somewhere, probably some young minister, since that was her father's profession.

Undaunted, Robert had waylaid Jenny the next afternoon as she left the building to ask her if she would like to go to the theatre with him the following evening.

"It's the local opera society's production of 'Carmen,' " he explained.

"Oh, yes! I saw it advertised. Thanks, Robert, I'd love to come,"

115

Jenny had said in her quiet, pleasant way, before hurrying off to the car park in an attempt to beat the rush-hour traffic.

★　　　★　　　★　　　★

Robert had stood stock still for several minutes, unable to believe his good fortune. Then when he had got home to his flat, he had sat down, even before his tea, and written a letter home to his family, just for the sheer pleasure of describing Jenny Blair and telling them she was going out with him.

It was only after he had posted the letter that he'd begun to have misgivings. What if Jenny never went out with him again? He would feel a bit of a fool.

Robert needn't have worried though. Jenny had accepted his next invitation — and his next . . .

"I knew you were different, the first morning you walked in the door," she told him with a happy sigh. "I kept hoping you would ask me out. Then telling myself I hadn't a chance with those two other pretty girls in the office."

"After I'd seen you I never noticed any other girls," Robert replied with perfect honesty.

Robert had never been as happy in his life before. Jenny was the perfect antidote for the harassments and frustrations of banking life. With her, every problem shrank to its proper size — he could overcome anything.

When she invited him to her home one evening he saw why. Jenny's father was minister of a church in the city's west side, and his manse was a red sandstone terrace-house overlooking a quiet little park. As soon as you walked in the door you were aware of a sense of orderliness and harmony.

Mrs Blair was Jenny in her mid-forties. Plumpish. Smiling. Calm and capable. And Jenny's father was a pale, bespectacled man whose smile lit up his face and whose gentle, lilting voice immediately made you feel that you could come to him for guidance with any problem whatsoever.

Jenny was an only child, and the three of them obviously loved one another very deeply. It was as simple as that.

Robert felt that he was accepted into the circle straightaway because he was Jenny's choice. And after the visit there was absolutely no need for Jenny to ask Robert if he liked her parents. She just knew he did. As she knew that they had liked Robert.

"And now you will have to come to Enterton with me and meet my family," Robert told her. "We'll make it a Saturday afternoon, shall we? Let's have a look at a few dates. Then I'll phone and see what suits them."

THE sixteenth of May then, Mum," Robert told his mother later that evening. "That's in a fortnight. All right?"

"Yes, dear, that's lovely." Mrs Parker's voice came and went on an exceptionally bad line. "We're really looking forward to

What An Introduction!

meeting Jenny. Gary's called the kitten after her."

"You didn't say you had a kitten," Robert shouted, as the line buzzed maddeningly.

"It's a stray," his mother yelled back. "Just a scrap."

"Look, this line's hopeless," Robert told her. "I'd best ring off, Mum. See you in a fortnight, then. Between two and three. Don't forget, now."

As he replaced the receiver he wished, half guiltily, that his father had answered the phone. Dad, a college lecturer, was the organiser of the family, whereas Mum, to put it kindly, was inclined to be absent-minded.

Whatever she was doing — home dressmaking, cardboard cut-outs for her Sunday school pupils, organising the village flower-show — it absorbed her completely. At these times the house was always full of the smell of burned potatoes. The fire had to be re-lit six times a day. And the dog began to look fat, because it often had two dinners — Robert had suspected even three in the past.

On the other hand, his father would check that the spare room was in order as soon as he knew a guest was coming, then lock the door on it in the meantime, so that the dog didn't lie on the clean bedcover, or Gary dump his gerbils' cage on the chest-of-drawers when the gerbils were evicted from his own room because of their noise.

However, on this occasion Robert had given Mum plenty of warning, so there shouldn't be any problem for him to worry about, he decided.

Robert told Jenny about his family on the drive down to Enterton.

"There's an eight-year-gap between me and Rosemary. She's fifteen. And Gary's twelve. After they had me, my parents went out to Africa to teach for seven years and it wasn't practical to have any more children until they were home again, you see.

"Rosemary's determined to be a writer. She spends her time composing poems and writing stories. Gary's the animal man. The house is like an animal rescue centre at times."

"They sound fun," Jenny said.

Robert looked out at the rainswept countryside and smiled wryly. Actually it was just on this kind of day that his family had sometimes driven him wild!

★ ★ ★ ★

The Parkers lived a little way out of the village in a bungalow with one not-very-large living-room, and if the weather was too bad for Gary and Rosemary to go out, they had all seemed to be on top of one another.

Robert used to sit in his bedroom for privacy, the bedroom that had been converted into a guest-room since he had left home two years ago. But today it would be different. They would be "ready for visitors," sitting with their best bibs and tuckers on, all agog to see Jenny.

"Gosh! You are out in the wilds!" Jenny exclaimed, as Robert turned to the right off the Enterton road and began to climb up a steep hill.

"Yes. Twelve miles from Pennock. That's our nearest town. Dad and Mum say they would rather have the braes and the burns than the benefits of civilisation on the doorstep."

A S they turned into the Parkers' driveway at precisely half-past two Robert saw to his disappointment that his father's car was gone from the garage.

He had hoped his family would all be together to meet Jenny. No doubt he had only dashed out for an errand, though. Some last-minute idea of Mum's.

He helped Jenny out of the car, and with his arm through hers, walked to the front door.

"I'll ring the bell. Like a real visitor," he said, eyes twinkling as he waited.

It needed two rings to bring Rosemary to the door, a notebook in one hand and blue Biro marks adorning her cheeks and nose, where her pen had rested as she looked for inspiration.

Her jaw dropped as she stared at her brother.

"What are you doing here?" She gasped after a moment. "It's next Saturday you're coming."

Robert experienced an unpleasant sinking feeling in the pit of his stomach.

"No, it's not, chicken," he said firmly. "It's today. Has there been a mix-up? Jenny . . . Rosemary. Rosemary . . . Jenny. Come on in, love," he added to his girlfriend.

Well, it might not be too bad, he told himself valiantly, as he pushed open the living-room door. There was a chance that Mum might be relaxing today.

★　　　★　　　★　　　★

She wasn't. The floor was carpeted with bits of material of varying sizes. And Mrs Parker was crawling over them, her mouth full of pins, and her hair tied back from her face with a piece of garden twine.

Gary lay sleeping on the settee with a tiny kitten purring on his stomach. And Rudy, the black retriever, was curled up in an armchair.

When Mrs Parker looked up and saw the visitors, she almost swallowed her pins. Replacing them in their box, she got slowly to her feet, her cheeks scarlet.

She smiled weakly at Jenny, then said, "Oh, no!"

"You forgot, Mum," Robert said tightly. "I can see that. Well, this is Jenny come to meet you. And Sleeping Beauty over there's my brother, Gary."

"He's having to feed the kitten every four hours. He's exhausted,"

Mrs Parker said, trying to remove the twine from her hair unobtrusively.

"Robert! I was *sure* you said you were coming next week," she added plaintively.

"Well, I didn't." Robert had rarely been so angry. This visit had been so important to him.

He hardly dared look at Jenny to see how she was taking it. When he did his worst fears were confirmed. Jenny was as straight-faced as he had ever seen her. In fact, she looked downright apprehensive as she took in the scene before her.

She hadn't spoken either since they came in, except to murmur a "How d'you do." She was obviously wondering what kind of people his family were.

"Where's Dad?" he asked shortly.

"He's away for the weekend," Rosemary cut in. "He's lecturing at a seminar. He thought you were coming next weekend. Like I said, we all did."

At this point Gary woke up, struggled into a sitting position and glared at them all. At first he looked as though he thought he was dreaming. Then he said in a strangled voice:

▶*over*

they were first...

THE star of the first talking picture, Al Jolson, was a sensational singer. That film — "The Jazz Singer" — was made in 1927 and during that hectic decade he was a worldwide smash. "Sonny Boy" — the song from his second film — gave him another first, as it was the first million-selling record from the "talkie" period.

He went on working right up to 1950 when he entertained American soldiers serving in Korea.

"There's nothing for them to eat, Mum! You said you wouldn't bother shopping until Monday since Dad was away. We've only got what's left of the ham. And that tiny tin of fruit."

"And the village shop's closed on a Saturday afternoon," Rosemary said, biting her lip.

"Gosh!" said Mrs Parker.

"Really, Mum!" Robert began angrily. Then he regained control of himself. "I'll drive over to Pennock to the supermarket," he said. "Are you coming, Jenny?"

"Don't be silly," his mother said. "She's only just arrived. Let her have a cup of tea and relax."

Robert looked at Jenny doubtfully. Her face was longer than ever. But he could think of nothing to say to his mother that wasn't downright rude.

"All right," he agreed shortly. "I'll be as quick as I can."

HE strode off into the kitchen to find a shopping bag. As he did so he happened to glance up at the calender-cum-diary on the wall above the tea-towels.

He could see where his mother had written in bright red pen, *Robert and Jenny,* and beneath it *23.* Only to begin with it had been *2-3.* He could see where the hyphen had been smudged.

She had written that down to remind her that they were arriving between two and three. And had looked at it a week later and thought it meant they were coming on the 23rd! But that wasn't all that dismayed him.

Beneath were all the preparations that had been planned for their coming.

Rosemary — cleaning of spare room. Flowers in vases. Writing ode of welcome.

Gary — help Mum with especially heavy shopping. Sweep path. Brush and comb Rudy in case of hairs.

Dad — Clean windows. Trim hedge. Cut grass.

Mum — Everything under the sun!

Robert had to swallow hard several times as he drove along the road to Pennock. That list had been a declaration of his family's love for him. And he had treated them shamefully this afternoon.

He loved Jenny dearly. But he loved them, too — no matter what she thought of them.

After he had bought the food at the supermarket in Pennock he did some conscience-shopping. A big bunch of flowers for his mother. A decent pen for Rosemary. And a box of whipped cream walnuts for his brother.

After some thought he added a couple of bottles of wine for his father.

When he arrived back he paused in the hallway for a few minutes. There was certainly a lot of chatter and laughter going on. He pushed open the living-room door to find Jenny down on the floor with his mother, doing mysterious things with pins to the pieces of cloth.

"I'm making a dress for your visit next week, if you want to know!" Mrs Parker exclaimed, when she spied Robert. "I've just been telling Jenny."

"I'm reading them my latest story while they work," Rosemary piped up.

"And I'm trying to hold back Rudy, because he wants to lick Jenny's face. And to control the kitten, because it wants to run up the curtain," Gary cried.

"And look out, Robert! Rudy's just seen you! He's coming!"

"Catch! Quickly!" Robert called, throwing the flowers to his mother, the pen to Rosemary and the sweets to Gary, before he received the affectionate attentions of one big, black dog.

Over Rudy's head he saw Jenny smiling at him. Radiantly.

★　　　★　　　★　　　★

"I couldn't have stood it if you'd been angry with them," Jenny explained to Robert as they walked along the quiet country road later that evening.

"They looked so busy and contented when we burst in on them. It gave me such a pleasant feeling." Jenny sighed. "A real family, I thought. And then you went all cold and horrid to them.

"I couldn't believe it was you. But then you came back with the flowers and everything, and I knew the real Robert Parker had come back."

Robert tried to explain. "I was so nervous. And you mean so much to me, Jen. I wanted my folk to make a good impression from the start . . ."

"They did," Jenny said.

A Mother's Gift

A MOTHER has the special gift of always speaking true,
A mother gets the praise or blame if skies be dark or blue.
Mother is sometimes a doctor, even a joiner or vet,
Jobs Mother cannot do have not been heard of yet.

A mother is a power all wise, a tyrant or a saint,
An oracle, a paragon with smart ideas or quaint.
Whatever else she may be, a mother knows full well,
A house could never be a home without her magic spell.

— Georgina Hall.

". . . because . . . well, I was intending to ask you rather an important question this weekend . . ."

"Really?"

"Can't you guess?"

"If the answer's 'yes,' will there be a family celebration, Robert?"

"Why do you think I bought Dad that wine?"

"Then let's go and tell your mum to have the corkscrew ready for his coming home," Jenny whispered, as Robert took her into his arms. □

In His Own

ANNA pulled the single sheet of paper from the typewriter. *Dear Mr Blake*, she read. *I'd be grateful if the electric kettle could be replaced. It doesn't heat up and I have been unable to make myself a drink all evening.*

The typing left something to be desired, Anna thought, noting the extended gaps between some letters. And, pen poised, she wondered if she should request a new machine also. However, as her parched throat reminded her of her craving for a cup of coffee, she decided that at this early stage she would give the kettle priority.

A. Darlington, she signed with a flourish, and propped the letter against the typewriter. Then she laid it flat again to add the words *thank you* above her signature.

Switching off all the lights, bar one over the counter, Anna moved towards the door into the street, pausing there to check that everything in the small office was in order.

The gaudy posters, lining the walls of the room, with their golden beaches, and blue seas and skies, looked almost believable in the dim light, and Anna experienced a stir of excitement.

Perhaps this summer she would be able to afford a holiday abroad — lie on such a beach, swim in such a sea. Maybe she'd even meet someone nice.

It wasn't that she was looking for a husband. What man would want to take on, not only her, but Betsy and Donald? Nice children though they were.

But . . . ? Her eyes strayed to another poster, where the sky was a deep midnight blue, and a handsome, tanned man smiled over his wine glass at a girl, equally brown, whose eyes reflected the light of the candle which stood on the table between them.

by PHYLLIS HEATH

122

Way

But . . . it would be lovely to dream, if only for the space of a fortnight.

Anna closed the door behind her, banging it slightly, not only to be sure it was secure, but also because she was angry, a little bit ashamed of her thoughts.

Dropping the keys into her bag and extracting her car keys, she set off towards the car park.

Though the travel agents branch office had occupied this same space for some years, modern development had caught up with it. Now a supermarket stood quite close and there was a space reserved for Anna's Mini, thus she hadn't far to walk. Not that she worried too much about being alone.

It was five years since she'd been widowed and she had got used to having to cope, but it was another thing which made this job so convenient. The hours, six until nine, five evenings a week, meant she could be there to have tea with nine-year-old Betsy and twelve-year-old Don — and be back home in time to tuck Betsy up for the night.

Weekends were free, too, and even the school holidays weren't any problem.

And I'll get staff discounts, Mr Middleton told me, she recalled, settling into her car. With what I'm earning now, we should be able to choose somewhere nice. So, now, if Mr Blake provides a new kettle, she chuckled, I won't have a care in the world.

HOWEVER, when she returned next evening there was no gleaming new kettle standing beside the tiny sink to greet her. There was a letter in the typewriter.

Mrs Darlington, I myself bring a vacuum flask, preferring ground coffee to instant. However, I have fitted a new element in said kettle. That was all that was needed.

There wasn't even a signature.

Anna tore the page from the machine.

"Said kettle! Ground coffee! What do you imagine I get paid for slaving away here?" she grumbled. "Why should I waste my money anyway, when there's instant provided? It's all right for you, Mr Blake, Sir! Mr *Manager* Blake, Sir! I'm just a lowly assistant. And if you'd been the one who'd interviewed me I wouldn't be that. For I wouldn't have taken the job if you'd offered it to me. So there!"

Reversing Mr Blake's note, Anna wound it back under the roller and began typing.

Dear Mr Blake. Thank you for repairing the kettle. I will endeavour, to the best of my ability, not to wear it out too quickly. Though I cannot guarantee not to use said kettle more than once each evening while the draught from under, and around, the office door continues to lower the temperature around me!

The roller squealed as she dragged out the letter, and her pen bit into the paper as she scrawled her name: *Anna Darlington.*

Next day she had some difficulty in opening the office door, and when she did manage, she saw a ribbon of draught excluder which ran up the edge and along the top — and a rubber strip which brushed the floor.

Anna's eyes gleamed with merriment.

Not waiting even to shed her coat, she ran to the corner table which housed the typewriter. Sure enough, there was a letter.

Dear Mrs Darlington. Your temperature appeared anything but low when you typed the note last night. However, the matter has been dealt with, and I trust everything is, now, to your satisfaction. Mr Middleton was insistent that you should receive every consideration.

A NNA chuckled. Mr Middleton was an old dear. There had been several very young, very with it, girls in the central office awaiting interviews along with herself.

As a result of Mr Middleton's consideration, this had been the first job where her age had been to her advantage. And when she had spoken of Betsy and Don, and the problems of working while giving them every care and attention, he had been most sympathetic.

"This is a family firm," he had told her. "My father began it, and my two brothers and I like to think we continue the way he would have wished us to. We look after our clients and we look after our staff, Mrs Darlington. Please remember that, my dear."

"Oh, I will, Mr Middleton. I will," Anna said, going back to open and shut the door once more and to run her hand down its edge, where the icy wind had been wont to whistle in, before Mr Blake's ministrations.

Dear Mr Blake, she tapped.

Anna was beginning to feel a little sorry for the way she had framed her previous reply.

It was most thoughtful of you to get the outer door draught-proofed. I do appreciate it. Now I won't have to wear my boots all evening, once winter arrives in full force, as I'd feared.

Nor buy thermal undies, she almost added, but quickly wound the paper out before she might be tempted.

Many thanks. Anna Darlington, she wrote instead.

As usual the reply was waiting for her next day.

My dear Mrs Darlington. Thank you for your note. T. Blake.

Brief and to the point, Anna thought, a little disappointed with its brevity, and with the fact that there seemed nothing else she could complain about. She had rather enjoyed the exchange, her mind forming a picture of T. Blake as the correspondence continued.

Thinning, silvery-grey hair, a long nose on which was perched round spectacles, she had decided. Tall, though maybe a little stooped, with large hands, and neat, precise movements. No extravagant gestures, for . . . Thomas?

Anna tried the other names she could recall beginning with T. Terence? Trevor? Timothy? No. Quite definitely Mr Blake was a Thomas, witness the "said" kettle, and the vacuum flask. Not to mention the ground coffee — freshly ground, no doubt.

She viewed the composite picture judiciously. Could there be a twinkle in the pale blue eyes? Recalling the dig about the temperature, Anna nodded. Yes, assuredly, a twinkle, even if it didn't shine all that often.

The short note seemed to be the end of the correspondence. It was a pity, really. It had been rather fun to come in each morning wondering what the typewriter might hold for her.

Dear Mr Blake, she typed, during a lull in business, then went back to squeeze in a T.

Business is booming, I'm pleased to say. But, if this keeps up, I might need an assistant. I could definitely use a new typewriter, she added, remembering that first letter. *A. D.*

Dear A. D.

Yes, he did have a sense of humour. Anna tugged out the paper with a grin.

I regret to tell you there will be no assistant and also, I'm afraid, no new typing machine; the present one is adequate for our needs, I'm sure you'll agree. But, as you say, business is booming, so, never fear, help is at hand. T. B.

A NNA read the note several times that evening, coming back to it whenever she had a spare moment.

The greeting had amused her, at first, but then he had gone on in his usual pedantic manner, irritating her somewhat. But, the part which brought a tingle of apprehension was the promise that help was at hand.

Studying the wording for the umpteenth time before checking that everything was in order before she left, Anna felt her apprehension increasing. There was only one conclusion she could put upon the words. Mr Thomas Blake — she was totally convinced he was a Thomas — was proposing to come to her aid himself. There was that telling phrase "our needs."

And he would scarcely be an assistant if he came into the bureau while she was here.

She wished she'd never mentioned the blessed typewriter. It was used for little else than their daily notes, and addressing the large envelopes into which she tucked enquiries for the people at head office to deal with.

During the drive home Anna grew quietly worried. She'd been enjoying having total control of the office. Her remarks about an assistant hadn't been totally serious. What she'd had in mind had been some young girl who might brew the coffee, and chat to clients while they were waiting for Anna's expert help — and slip out to the takeaway, on those occasions when a domestic crisis had left Anna supperless.

Somehow, she couldn't envisage Mr T. Blake in any of these roles — even if he did have a sense of humour. Not the man who wrote of said kettles and typing machines.

Through that night, and all next day, she tussled with the wording of her next letter, and by the time the next evening was over she thought she had it right.

Dear T. B. Your letter brought to my notice the fact that there are only very occasional letters to be typed. Perhaps I was presumptuous in requesting a new machine, especially when as a family concern, the firm might not be in a position to welcome such an expense. As to the question of extra staff, I do pride myself on giving our cust . . .

She crossed out that word with a series of X s and substituted "clients" . . .*my personal attention. So I'm sure you will agree there is no need to put yourself to any expense or trouble on my behalf.* Anna she signed with a flourish.

His reply was waiting for her when she arrived next evening. It had been taken from the machine and lay in the centre of the desk. He had even signed it with a pen — though she couldn't decipher the names — an unusual occurrence which spoke of him having taken more time.

Normally, she knew, he left the premises at four-thirty sharp. There had been talk of her starting work before he left, but that had been out of the question. Today, it didn't look as if he'd dashed off the note, one eye on the clock, before putting on his overcoat and leaving to catch his bus.

Dear Anna, Thank you for your concern, both for the firm's welfare and for mine. However, I confirm what I said in my previous letter. Help is at hand. The new equipment will be installed shortly and, of course, a demonstration will be given you in its operation. I'm sure you will find it a great help.

Anna sighed. There was only one thing this new equipment could be — a computer! Hadn't she seen them in every other travel agent she'd ever entered?

Help, as T. Blake said, was at hand. There would be no more endless delays while she tried to get a line through to head office. No more need for would-be clients to check back with her. No more endless records to be kept, copied, and forwarded to head office.

Everything would be done by this wonderful machine, at the touch of a button. Well, at the touch of several buttons, Anna supposed.

There was only one problem left, as far as she could see — and that was she had no idea at all which buttons she would have to touch!

Her son, Don, at twelve, talked knowledgeably about soft and hardware, input and output, computer language, visual display units, and memories, but it was all Greek to his mother. The thought of a computer installed right here, in this office, made her tremble.

I'll leave, was her first thought. I'll give in my notice.

But then she remembered the holiday she had booked for the three of them. She'd never be able to afford it if she wasn't earning, never mind the added savings of the staff discount. Yet, how could she deprive Betsy and Don? They were so looking forward to it.

She couldn't! Somehow she was going to have to get along with this monster, others did.

Anna left the office that evening without typing even a short note of thanks. She didn't feel she had anything to thank him for.

THERE was a slight reprieve — a week when she carried on as she'd always done, savouring each task, enjoying her uncomplicated existence. But, one evening, she walked into the bureau to find the computer waiting for her.

She walked round the television screen, eyeing it distrustfully. But, as it remained blank she realised it wasn't switched on. Well, at least she wasn't to be called upon to use it just yet.

At a quarter to six the telephone rang.

"Mrs Darlington?"

Anna acknowledged her name.

"Would it be convenient if I came along and showed you round the computer? You're not too busy, just now?"

"No, there's no-one here. I expect it's the weather." Anna didn't want to give this stranger the impression that the office wasn't normally buzzing with people.

"Fine! Yes, it is a terrible night, a real stinker! Maybe no-one will turn out and we can really get to grips . . . well, you know what I mean."

Anna found herself laughing. Perhaps it wouldn't be so bad, after all. This young man sounded pleasant and easy going. Clearly he wasn't expecting her to know everything, or even anything, she amended.

"Yes, I know what you mean. I'll switch the kettle on. I'm sure you'll be glad of a cup of coffee by the time you arrive."

She was glad she had prepared coffee as the man who walked into the bureau some thirty minutes later looked distinctly wet.

He shed his anorak with a wry smile, shaking the rain off it as he stood on the mat.

"Sorry about this." Flinging back the dark hair from his forehead, he took off his glasses and began to polish them on a tissue.

"Won't be a sec, I'm all steamed up. I keep saying I'll get contact lenses, but it seems like vanity at my age."

"But . . ." Anna began to protest that he wasn't old, about her own age, she would have guessed, maybe a year or two older.

"I'll get the coffee," she said instead, turning back into the little room.

When she came back, carrying two steaming mugs, the man was standing over the computer.

"Know anything about these toys?" he asked.

"Well, no, not really. In fact." She laughed, a little nervously. "I'm not keen on the idea of having one, but . . . Mr Blake seems to think it's necessary."

"Mister . . . ?" The man turned. "Sorry, I didn't think. We haven't met, have we, Mrs Darlington . . . ? It is Mrs Darlington, isn't it?"

In His Own Way

"Yes, of course! Who else were you expecting? Didn't Mr Blake explain?"

"I'm Tony Blake."

"You're Mr Blake? Oh! Oh, and I gave you instant coffee!"

It was the first thing that came into Anna's head and she blushed as she saw how ridiculous it must sound.

"You — you said you brought a flask," she stuttered. "I thought maybe your wife filled it for you."

"I'm not married . . . leastways, not now . . . Those letters . . . you sounded different, not a bit like you . . . look," he ended.

"T. B." Anna spluttered. "I thought the T. was for Thomas. You sounded like a Thomas."

"And you sounded . . . Well, all that about being cold and wearing boots . . ."

Anna lifted one shapely leg for his inspection and Tony just had time to admire the short, up-to-the-minute boots she was wearing before she replaced it beside its partner.

"I'm sorry," Tony Blake said, as if he really thought it was his fault that he should think of her as an old woman.

"You and your said kettle! No wonder I took you for . . . I did decide you had a sense of humour." She laughed, as embarrassment coloured her cheeks once more.

"Maybe we'd better get on with showing you how this works," Tony said, watching the blush fade.

★　　　★　　　★　　　★

He was a good instructor, and he didn't make Anna feel at all stupid for not understanding everything, right away. In fact, she rather enjoyed her lessons and was sorry she couldn't have been just a little stupid so that Tony might have to come back again.

When she was leaving he walked her to her car.

"I'm not sure I like the idea of you doing this alone," he told her, glancing around the almost empty precinct. "Maybe I'll drop in some evenings, just to be sure you have understood everything." He grinned. "Mr Middleton does always say we must take care of our staff."

Anna smiled. "Well, no more letters, at least," she told him, getting into her seat.

"Mmm! I'll rather miss them. Messages on the computer's memory aren't quite the same thing. Perhaps I will call in more often."

There was one letter . . .

Anna found it propped against the ancient typewriter some months later.

Dearest A. D., it read. *Couldn't we change that to A. B? Mrs Anthony Blake (in case you're in any doubt).*

But Anna didn't think she needed to reply. By this time A. D. and T. B. knew each other very well. □

THE HAND OF FRIENDSHIP

E LLA GREENSIT didn't usually visit the town twice in one week. There were bus fares, the inevitable cup of coffee, or if she felt very reckless, lunch. Ever since Tuesday though, the memory of the dress had teased at her until she felt she had to see if it was still there. If it had been sold . . . well, that would settle it.

So Thursday found Ella standing in front of the gown shop in the High Street. The dress was just as she remembered it. Delicate dusky pink, ruching round the heart-shaped neck and deep-buttoned cuffs. How Sam would have loved it.

Ella's thoughts drifted back to her wedding day almost fifty years before. Her dress had been exactly that shade and Sam had whispered that she looked like a newly-opened rose.

She smiled. She would have to think hard to find another occasion when Sam found either the words or the courage to pay her such a compliment. Nevertheless he had been a good, caring husband and she still missed him, although she had been alone for over five years.

Lost in thought she didn't notice the girl standing beside her and when she heard a dreamy voice murmur, "Isn't it a lovely dress?" she nodded and agreed that it was.

Only then did the young woman and the elderly lady look at each other. Simultaneously they realised they each were talking about a different dress, and their laughter bubbled out.

Ella looked at the simple green shift dress, lightened only by the bold embroidery across the bodice.

"It would suit you," she told the girl.

"Mmm, I know! That pinky one is just your colour as well," the girl said wistfully. Then her eyes lit up.

"How about trying them on? We could go in together then we wouldn't feel so bad walking out."

"Oh!" Ella, not used to such sudden suggestions, especially from strangers, was taken aback. Then she saw the twinkle in the girl's eyes.

"Come on," the girl persuaded, "I hate trying things on alone. I'm

130

by
MARY
SHEPHERD

such easy meat for a salesgirl, even when things don't suit me. I'm Grace Morden, by the way. I'm also perfectly harmless, I can assure you."

The girl's friendliness was infectious and Ella found herself holding out a hand.

"Ella Greensit — and I think I'll be very naughty and try the dress on."

Not very wise, Ella, she told herself as they stepped into the communal dressing-room. Especially when she had the money for her electricity bill in her purse.

E LLA needn't have worried. The shoulder pads stood out from her small-boned shoulders, the waist was definitely in the wrong place and the neck, modest on the window model, was certainly not modest on Ella Greensit.

She looked at Grace, saw her trying not to laugh and laughed at herself. But their chuckles died down as Grace slipped into the green shift. It was perfect — with or without the optional belt.

"Oh, Grace! It looks lovely."

Grace grimaced.

"I knew it would be fatal to try it on! Oh, Ella, I shouldn't!" she exclaimed.

"It isn't really *that* expensive," Ella pointed out. "Certainly not as dear as my creation."

"Even so . . . Oh, blow it! It might be ages before I find anything as nice. I'll take it."

As they left the shop Ella suggested coffee together.

"My treat," she told Grace. "Out of the money I've saved on my dress!"

Only when they were seated did she realise that Grace might not have the time to waste over coffee — that she might have other things she wanted to do.

Grace smiled in answer to her query.

"No! I've plenty of time. Too much," she added ruefully. "We only moved here from down south a few weeks ago and I miss my family and friends. To make things worse, ours is the first house on the estate to be occupied and we're surrounded by empty shells.

"Of course that will change, and when other people move in . . . well, there are bound to be other young wives and mothers."

"You've got children then?" Ella asked as she stirred brown sugar into the frothy coffee.

Grace blushed, then gave the infectious grin Ella was beginning to look for.

"Oh! I might as well tell you! If I don't tell someone I think I will explode! Mick and I have been wanting a family for ages. There have been a few disappointments, but this morning I have been for a test. The doctor is sure I'm pregnant but I'll have to go to the hospital for a further test.

"I don't want to tell Mick until then so it's a good job he's away. He travels a good bit for his firm. As soon as I'm sure about it I'll put on a special meal and wear my new dress! I can't wait!"

Happiness radiated from her, and Ella leaned across the table and covered her slim hand with her own.

"I do hope things work out well for you, my dear! What a pity I won't know!"

"But I'd like you to! Why don't we meet here a week from today? My treat next time!" She laughed.

After she had gone, Ella treated herself to a second cup of coffee and sat for a while thinking. She knew about loneliness. It was a few months now since she had reluctantly left the rather large terraced house she had shared with Sam.

Oh, she liked her small modern flat, but she missed her old friends. The flats above her were occupied by two sisters. Although they had a flat each, they were obviously content with each other's company and Ella, her friendly overtures apparently rebuffed, soon retreated into her shell.

Martha Towers in the flat opposite was partially crippled, but when Ella had proffered help the old lady had bristled with indignation.

Ella knew herself to be shy with new people, slow to open out, so she was surprised how easily she had fallen into conversation with Grace.

The Hand Of Friendship

On an impulse she called into a small wool shop on her way home and bought some pale yellow wool. If Grace's hopes were dashed, a sale of work was always glad of baby clothes.

B Y Wednesday morning, the day before she was due to meet Grace, the matinée coat was finished. Ella pressed it and spread it out to cool before wrapping it in soft tissue.

She was just putting the ironing board away when there was an agitated knock at the door. To Ella's surprise, Aileen Clayton, one of the upstairs sisters, stood there.

"Oh, Mrs Greensit! I am sorry but — but well, my sister left her bathroom tap running and flooded the bathroom. We're so worried the water may have seeped through to your ceiling!"

Followed by an anxious Aileen, Ella walked quickly to the bathroom. They gazed upwards and both heaved sighs of relief.

"All clear so far," Ella said. "It was kind of you to come and tell me though. Thanks."

"Not at all, it would have been awful if your ceiling had fallen down. Oh! How pretty!"

Aileen picked up the little baby coat. "For one of your grandchildren?"

"No, just for a friend. She has only just moved up here and is

▶over

ON the morning of May 4, 1979, history was made in Britain when we woke to discover we had elected our first woman Prime Minister, Margaret Thatcher.

Seen here with her husband, Dennis, shortly after that triumph, Mrs Thatcher went on to win two more General Elections, in 1983 and 1987. A former research chemist, Mrs Thatcher first entered Parliament in 1959, winning the seat of Finchley.

they were first...

missing her family and friends her own age. Thought it would cheer her up."

"It's lovely! But Sally is still mopping up so I'll have to go and help."

The two ladies smiled companionably at each other as Ella opened the door, and Ella hummed contentedly as she finished tidying up.

A little later there was another knock at the door, and when Ella opened it both sisters were standing there.

Aileen held out a small, cheeky white rabbit.

"My sister and I make these. I thought your friend might like one."

"Oh, how kind!" Ella hadn't time to say more. The sisters were already moving away.

"Sorry, but we can't linger. It's the Ladies' Guild! It is our turn for the teas. Perhaps you would like to join us sometime?" Aileen called back to her.

Ella's day of surprises was not over, though. The sisters had hardly left when she heard the sound of breaking glass in the hall. Martha Towers stood looking down at the flood of milk and the broken glass. She stooped to begin to clear it, but Ella stopped her.

"No, really, Mrs Towers. You must let me! It is too dangerous. You might cut yourself or overbalance. Look, come and sit in my flat a few minutes while I clear your doorway."

Somewhat reluctantly Martha allowed Ella to sit her in an armchair while she busied herself clearing away the broken glass. When Ella came back she put the kettle on and handed Martha a cup of tea, silencing her protests.

"No, you look as though you need it. You know, Martha, it is often harder to accept a bit of help than to give it."

The old lady gave her a thoughtful look, then nodded to the baby things still on the settee.

"See you've been busy."

So Ella told her about Grace Morden, and how Sally Clayton had flooded the bathroom.

"Feel how soft it is," she said, handing her guest the furry rabbit.

Was there a glint of tears in Martha's old eyes, wondered Ella, but she said nothing as Martha struggled to her feet.

"I must go now! The welfare lady will be calling. Er . . . thank you for helping me!"

For once Martha didn't argue when Ella handed her a jug of milk, assuring her she could easily spare it.

The next morning as Ella was getting ready she heard Martha shuffling across the hall and then knock at her door.

"Here!" Martha held out a small box. "For the baby! Nothing much, just an old silver threepenny bit. I kept some and have given all my nieces and nephews one."

She turned away, brushing aside Ella's thank you.

Ella opened the box. The small silver piece nestled in a bed of cotton wool. Ella recalled the days when, long ago, she had held a

The Hand Of Friendship

threepenny piece in her hand as she pressed her nose to the sweet-shop window.

A threepenny bit was a small fortune then — it was more often a halfpenny, she thought, smiling, as she put the box carefully into her handbag.

THERE was no need to ask Grace about the results of the test. Her smile said it all.

"Mick is so thrilled! Look! I've left a casserole in the oven. I hoped you might come home with me and share it. Then I can show you the baby's room."

So they left the coffee-room together and Grace drove Ella back with her.

"Why, it is quite near where I live!" Ella told her. "Only about twenty minutes' walk."

"Just a nice stroll with a pram," Grace grinned. "How are you at baby minding?" she teased.

Ella's heart was warm as she assured her young friend she was quite able to cope. Grace was thrilled with the presents. and very touched by the kindness of people she had not even met.

"There's a cake here I've just made. Take it and give everyone a piece."

Grace drove Ella home but wouldn't go in.

"Another time. Mick will be home for a meal and when he's away so much I like to be there if possible."

Once indoors Ella eyed the cake thoughtfully. Then she went upstairs and knocked at the door of one of the flats.

Aileen and Sally Clayton were together and Ella passed on Grace's thanks.

"She sent us a cake to share. I could bring you some up here but I wondered . . . if I put the kettle on, would you join me?"

For a moment there was silence, then for once Sally took the lead.

"Thank you, Ella! That would be very nice. Shall we say fifteen minutes?"

It took more courage to knock at Martha Towers' door.

"Grace said to thank you for the silver piece. She is sure it will bring the baby luck and she is going to put it on a little bracelet.

"She also sent us a cake to share. Sally and Aileen Clayton are going to have theirs with me. Would you join us, Martha? Please?"

For a few minutes Martha looked at her visitor. Had she detected pity, Ella knew she would have refused, but finally the old lady nodded.

"That will make a nice change," she said quietly. "Thank you!"

Back in her own room, Ella spread a lace cloth on the small table and laid out her best china. Her eyes went to Sam's photograph on the sideboard.

"It was a lucky dress after all, Sam," she whispered. "See how many friends it has brought me. Now I'd better put the kettle on. The neighbours are coming to tea." □

by SUE DICKS

INTO THE SUNSHINE

"A UNTIE, can I wear this one?"
Carol looked to see what her
eight-year-old niece had chosen
from the jewels and trinkets on her
dressing-table. Her heart leapt when
she saw Lucy was holding the gold
locket.

She should have put that away
before promising the child she could
have whichever one she wanted for
the morning. Still, a promise must be
kept, and she was very anxious to
make this special visit a success.

"Of course you can, darling," she
said with an effort. "But you must be
very careful with it. It's one of the
most precious things I've got."

Lucy's eyes opened wide. "Did it
cost lots of money?"

Carol smiled. "I doubt it. It
belonged to my grandmother — your

mummy's grandmother, too, of course, but I was ill for a long time when I was little so I went to stay with her and she called me her 'special' grandchild."

Even now, she felt nostalgia for the happy, flower-filled convalescence in the old country house. Her grandmother, whom she adored, had given her a lifelong love of the country and gardens.

"She used to wear it every day," she explained to Lucy, "because her husband had given it to her. I used to love to play with it and wear it, just like you!

"She gave it to me just before she died and now it's what I have to remember her by. Look, I've put a photo of her in it."

On one side of the opened locket was a sepia portrait of an old lady with white hair piled high, and an upright lace collar. Lucy looked with even more interest at the modern picture on the other side.

"Who's that?" she asked.

Carol tried to speak casually, to sound relaxed, but it was hard even after all this time. She never opened the locket to show anyone. However, she knew her sister, Isobel, had told the child everything about the events of five years ago.

"It's Laura — my own little girl," she said simply.

"Ooh!" Lucy peered even more closely at the tiny coloured photo of a golden-haired toddler. "She was ever so pretty!"

"Yes, she was," Carol replied gently. "Now, come on, let's put it round the neck of another pretty little girl!"

Lucy giggled with pleasure at the flattery, and managed to stand still for ten seconds while her aunt carefully did up the fine gold chain.

Several times that morning the little girl broke off from her playing and opened the round, engraved locket to look at the photos. She seemed quite happy pottering about the tiny cottage, but was even more enthusiastic about the garden.

"Where are the flowers, Auntie?" she suddenly asked.

Carol laughed and pointed at the lilac.

Lucy frowned.

"That's a tree," she informed her. "I mean proper flowers, that come out of the ground."

"They need looking after. I have shrubs and trees instead because I haven't got time for much gardening."

THIS wasn't the whole truth. Her husband, Norman, had loved flowers as she had — indeed, they had first met when he had generously come to look after her grandmother's garden when the old lady became ill.

It was there, in the orchard one blossom-laden spring, that he had finally proposed to her. They had planned to have their own garden just as beautiful, and they had succeeded.

In the car accident, both Norman and three-year-old Laura had been killed outright. For her own two months in hospital, Carol had been in benumbed shock.

Then, when she went home, she saw their garden. Those flowers that still flourished filled her with unbearable nostalgia, and those that had died — like all Norman's beloved greenhouse blooms — had given her a pain even more acute.

Carol had wept then, as never before or since, and at last the long, slow healing had begun. Everyone admired the courage with which she had rebuilt her life. Just a few aspects of it remained untried territory still — and growing more flowers was one of them.

By lunch time, Carol could see Lucy was growing restless.

"Would you like to come down to the village shop with me this afternoon?" she asked her while they were eating their meal.

"Yes, please!" Lucy cheered up instantly. "I like shopping. Shall I take my pocket money? Daddy gave me a new purse."

"I doubt if you'll find much to buy here! Take it by all means, but we'll go into town if you want to look at the bigger shops."

Carol noticed that when Lucy was excited, she fidgeted, pulling at the locket she still wore round her neck. She made a mental note to make sure they took it off before they went out, in case it fell off somewhere unnoticed.

In the end, they both went out in a carefree mood. They walked down the narrow village street which basked in the early afternoon sun. Lucy looked at everything with curiosity and smiled at everyone.

Carol watched her running ahead with a growing feeling of warmth and affection.

She and Isobel had always been close, and her sister had tried hard to help at the time of the tragedy. But she had had a daughter the same age — Lucy and Laura had even started to play together on visits — and, more, was expecting another child.

Carol deeply appreciated her family's support, but the only way she could cope at that time was by avoiding other children.

Isobel had understood this very sensitively, but Carol knew she still cherished the hope that her sister and daughter would become close. Especially after her own tragedy.

Isobel's second child, a son, had been born severely handicapped. Carol had tried to help in her turn, but still tended to withdraw from children.

Now, Isobel and Owen had the chance of a week abroad for his firm. It would be their first holiday since poor little Danny's birth. Danny would go back happily into hospital, but Lucy . . .

Of course, Carol said she would have her.

"Just for a long weekend at first," Isobel urged. "Get used to each other. If it doesn't work, we'll forget about it."

Carol felt she'd agree to anything to give her sister and brother-in-law such a well-deserved holiday.

THEY reached the little village shop and while she was buying provisions from Wilma, the friendly shopkeeper on whom the whole village depended, Carol heard Lucy whoop excitedly.

"Can I buy some of these, Auntie?"

They turned to see Lucy fingering a row of packets of flower seeds.

Wilma laughed delightedly. "That's a good thing to see a child wanting to buy! Mind you," she added with her usual honesty, "you'll get a better selection at that new nursery that's opened down by the main road."

She turned to Carol with a conspiratorial smile.

"They say he's very nice, the chap who's running it," she went on. "Good looker he is, too, I'd say. And a young widower."

Carol's mood changed. She hated these clumsy attempts to matchmake for her. Couldn't they just leave her in peace?

"There are plenty of seed packets here, thank you," she said sharply, and went to help Lucy choose.

"Could I plant them in your garden when I get home?" Lucy pleaded. "Please! That's where I want to put them!"

Her aunt had to agree, and they settled for marigolds, the brightest colour packet in the shop.

All the way home, Lucy was excited, stopping only to try the swings on the village green. Watching her sail upwards, Carol saw a flash of gold in the sun. The locket! They'd

If No-one Called

SOMEONE may come to call when you are turning out a room,
With things all topsy turvy while you're wielding mop and broom;
With a flash of irritation, replaced by rueful grin,
You maybe wish them miles away though you invite them in.

Yet think how dull your life would be if no-one came to call,
How extra loud would seem the ticking clock upon the wall.
Be ready then to welcome friends whenever they drop in,
It doesn't matter if the house isn't like a shining pin.
If no-one called and you were left alone upon the shelf,
It's certain you would very soon be talking to yourself!

— *Georgina Hall*

forgotten to take it off! Ah well, they were nearly home.

It was in the front garden that they found space, and Lucy soon learnt how to plant out the tiny, curled seeds.

Carol remembered the musty smell and vibrant colours of the old English Marigolds that had tumbled over the front path at her grandmother's. She looked round the restrained front garden of her own cottage, with its formal evergreens.

Thoughtfully, she went in to make some tea while Lucy carried on, muddy and contented.

After only a few minutes, she heard a scream and rushed out.

Lucy ran sobbing towards her.

"Th-the locket!" She gasped. "It's not on m-me any more! I've lost it! It must've f-fallen off!"

Taken unawares, Carol couldn't hide her own dismay. She would rather have lost anything but that.

"I'm sorry," the poor child continued, her face contorted with fresh sobs when she saw her aunt's reaction.

Carol remembered something else her sister had said. "Lucy needs a break from Danny, too. She's had to be old for her years, bless her. She helps such a lot, and it's made her very kind and considerate."

Why then should she be upset now, Carol thought, because an adult was living in the past?

"It's all right," she urged, holding the sobbing child to her. "It was *my* fault, not yours. You've done nothing wrong."

"Can't we go and look for it?" Lucy sniffed, only half consoled by Carol's words.

THEY looked everywhere, especially round the swings, but found nothing.

"That's enough," Carol said firmly, sounding more cheerful than she felt. "We won't find it, and it really doesn't matter."

She tried to interest Lucy again in the garden and various games, but the day had lost its lustre.

"Will they be flowers before I go home?" the little girl asked, looking hopefully at the bare earth under which her precious seeds lay.

"Oh, darling, they take weeks to grow and you go home in two days!"

Carol laughed gently as she looked down at the disappointed little face.

"I tell you what," she said impulsively, "we could go to that garden centre Wilma told us about and find some plants that are — well, already grown up. Then we can have flowers for the weekend!"

Lucy was immediately excited, and very soon they were in the nursery looking at rows of plants set out on the new benches. Carol found old memories were stirring — also some new enthusiasms.

"What are those called?" Lucy pointed to a row of greyish shrubs.

"Lavender," Carol told her. "You can have a row of them and they make a lovely hedge full of purple flowers," she went on eagerly. "In fact, one would look very nice along my front path!"

"That's an excellent idea!"

Carol wheeled round to see a man answering Wilma's description, who'd obviously been listening to what she'd just said.

It turned out he was indeed Ewan Downs, the owner of the new centre.

In the afternoon sun, surrounded by the plants she knew and loved and interrupted by Lucy's chatter, she found it easy to talk. They fell to swopping notes on the various village gardens.

"Is yours the last white cottage before the stream?" Ewan asked.

She nodded, silently wondering how he knew where she lived.

"Well, I must say I agree with you about the lavender hedge," he continued. "I have a delivery of some fresh plants this evening, good Dwarf Munstead, that would be ideal. Why not wait until they come?"

He spoke with an infectious cheerfulness and had the healthy good looks of someone used to working in the open air.

That being apparently settled, they bought some colourful bedding plants for Lucy's sake and the two of them returned home. Once Lucy had dug enormous holes for her begonias, she stood back to admire her work.

"It looks more pretty now, doesn't it?"

Carol willingly admitted that it did, and again left Lucy outside while she went to start supper in the kitchen. This time, it was the sound of a man's voice with Lucy's that sent her hurrying back out.

I WAS just passing on my way home," Ewan Downs explained, "and having a most interesting conversation with the young gardener here!

"Look —" He broke off suddenly. "Is that buried treasure?"

A gleam of gold lay beside some long grass, and Lucy and Carol both fell on it with an eagerness that took him by surprise. It was the locket. So it had only fallen off in the garden after all!

All was undamaged except for Laura's photograph; that had fallen off and was torn and stained.

Carol fingered the empty half of the locket and found a few strands of the tiny lock of hair that had been behind the picture. How strange to touch it again.

She looked up to meet Ewan's eyes. He was watching her keenly while he listened to Lucy's rather garbled version of the story.

"I also wanted to tell you the lavender has come," he said at last. "Would you like me to bring some round for you tomorrow morning, to save you the journey?"

"Tomorrow!" exclaimed Lucy. "That's soon, isn't it? That's the day it is when I wake up the next day!"

It was impossible to say no after that, and Carol heard herself add, "Why not make it coffee time?"

Later in the evening, she remembered this with considerable surprise. She couldn't regret it, though, and she realised it was a long time since she had wanted to find out more about a new acquaintance who was still a stranger to her.

Maybe it wasn't only flowers she should allow to grow in her life again . . .

"Have you got another photo of Laura?" Lucy suddenly asked. She had crept on to her aunt's lap.

"Yes, I have." Carol spoke quietly and stroked her hair. "And I've got a big one the same as the one that was in the locket."

"Why don't you put it in a frame and have it on the mantelpiece?"

Why not? How did you explain to a child?

"It would be nice for everyone to see it," Lucy went on regardless. "Better than — well, than sort of locking it away inside something."

Carol thought for a long time before looking down into her niece's eyes.

"You're right," she said at last. "Tomorrow you can help me find a frame for it."

Lucy leant contentedly against her aunt's shoulder.

"And do you know what?" Carol continued after a while. "Can you guess whose photo I'm going to put in the locket now?"

The child shook her head sleepily.

"Yours, if you'll let me," she said softly. Granny would approve. She smiled to herself — two gardeners together!

The expression on Lucy's face was answer enough.

"I expect Mummy's got lots you can have," she assured her confidently.

"That reminds me," Carol exclaimed, sitting up. "We said we'd ring Mummy. Do you want to speak to her?"

"Yes, please!"

"What will you tell her?"

Lucy thought quickly. "All about my happy day!" she decided.

Carol bent to kiss her.

"I'll tell her about mine, too!" she said with conviction. □

THE pioneer of television, John Logie Baird, was born in Helensburgh in 1888. As a young man, he began his research into television and in 1926 succeeded in giving the first demonstration.

Today, with colour television and satellite links bringing us programmes from the other side of the world, it's easy to forget, in this the centenary of his birth, how much we owe to this Scot.

they were first...

HIS lips against hers were cool. His moustache tickled slightly. His arm was heavy across her shoulder. But although she was aware of these physical sensations, Eleanor knew that none of them affected her.

She felt no emotion whatsoever. And a kind of basic honesty prompted her to speak.

"You know, Keith, I think we might as well say that this is our last date."

Keith Cameron dragged his arm swiftly from around her and stared at her with an expression which bordered on alarm.

"What do you mean, Eleanor?" he asked in a clipped tone of voice. "What's on your mind?"

"Nothing . . ." She paused, perplexed by his reaction, then she continued in a strained voice.

"All I meant was that we seem to have gone stale on each other these past few weeks. We've hardly exchanged a word tonight, for instance. So I thought . . ." She halted and shrugged, waiting for him to comment. When he didn't she said irritably:

That Wonderful Moment

by PEGGY MAITLAND

144

"Just because your brother married my sister, and we were bridesmaid and best man, that doesn't mean that you have to escort me everywhere for the rest of my life!"

"Are you saying we should stop seeing each other?" Keith asked.

He sounded amazed, Eleanor thought. And at the same time pleased, she was certain. Then his eyes definitely brightened and he

straightened his wide shoulders as his features relaxed into a smile.

It was days later before Eleanor realised that he had displayed symptoms of relief.

"I'd let him off the hook, you see," Eleanor told her mother, after describing their parting.

"Then you don't mind about this other girl he was seen with?" Mrs Aitken enquired hesitantly.

"No. But I'm glad you told me." Eleanor smiled, and patted her mother's hand.

"I suppose I ought to have told you that we'd decided to call it a day," she went on, "but it didn't seem that important — especially when you were rushing around organising the house for Janet coming home."

"Was it that same night?" Mrs Aitken was sympathetic and she felt vaguely guilty, as if she had failed her younger daughter somehow. The end of a romance was always sad, she thought.

However, now Eleanor was changing the subject, her tone and her expression indicating very clearly that she'd had enough of confiding in her mother.

M RS AITKEN had dreaded telling Eleanor that Keith Cameron was going out with another girl. But as they lived in a small town, news like that always got around — although it was often slow to arrive at the ears of the person most concerned!

"I was afraid that Eleanor would be hurt," Mrs Aitken told her elder daughter later.

But Janet was more irritated than sympathetic.

"I suppose that means we won't be seeing Keith," she said and since she had been depending on him to give her transport, she added, "I'll have to go on the bus to visit my in-laws."

"You don't look fit to do much visiting," Mrs Aitken said. "We could invite them here, if you think that would be better."

"Maybe that would be awkward, too." Janet heaved a deep sigh and said wistfully, "I wish I'd gone to America with George. I'm sure I would have been fine once I got there. The baby isn't due for another five weeks."

"Now, Janet," Mrs Aitken said briskly, "you mustn't start fretting, it isn't good for the baby."

"Or I could have stayed in the flat by myself," Janet continued glumly. "At least I would have been surrounded by all my own furniture and things."

"But George thought that you'd be better with us," Mrs Aitken reminded her, "and we are pleased to have you home again."

And then soothingly she went on, "It used to be a tradition, you know. Girls always returned to their family home to have their first baby. I know that you'll be back in Glasgow and George will be home before yours is due — but still, it's a nice idea, isn't it?"

Janet raised a small smile as she answered.

"Coming home to Mother is nice in a way — you are spoiling me and I admit I'm enjoying it, but . . ." She sighed again.

"I would never willingly be separated from George . . . I do miss him."

And then as her sister, Eleanor, came into the room, she gave her a rueful grin. "I'm moaning again. Mum must be fed up listening to me."

Eleanor returned her sister's smile.

"Well, I hope it's given you an appetite because Dad and I have finished cutting the hedges and we are about to make a mountain of cheese and toast," she said brightly.

Working outside had soothed Eleanor's troubled mind to some extent. But she remained deeply sorry for her sister. Poor Janet, she kept thinking.

Only a year ago she was a happy bride imagining that she and George would enjoy a rosy future. And now George had hopped off on some business trip to America leaving Janet alone and more miserable than she had ever been in her life.

As for Janet's pregnancy, Eleanor was dismayed and distressed by her sister's appearance. A slight bump in the middle was usual, she had thought, but Janet's entire body was swollen and her face was blotched and puffy.

No wonder there are permanent tears in her eyes, Eleanor thought. But she made a determined effort to keep Janet from moping too much. Eleanor did not quite admit it to herself, but her involvement with her sister helped to keep

▶*over*

Springtime Remembered

ON dreamy April eves, do you recall
   Those bygone springs, when you and I
were small?
When, just like magic, overnight
Wild cherry trees turned dazzling white,
And little charming primrose faces
Glimmered in green woodland places?

When pussy-willow, silver-grey,
And lambs'-tails, decked the woodland way,
And chestnut's "sticky-buds" would fill
Tall jars on cluttered window-sill?
While tadpoles, banished to the shed,
Were lad's delight — and mother's dread!

Where have they gone, dear days of old,
Of cowslips' freckled, fairy gold,
Of blackbirds singing in the rain?
We thought they'd never come again,
Yet, blossom-pink and sparkling blue,
Each year they still return — anew!
— *Kathleen O'Farrell*

her thoughts away from Keith Cameron. We cooled off, she would remind herself sternly. There is no point in letting yourself regret his absence from your life.

WHEN Keith came to the house to see her sister, Eleanor skilfully avoided him. But one night he was waiting for her outside the library where she worked.

"Can I give you a lift home?" he asked her at once.

He looked and sounded worried and tense.

Eleanor's thoughts flew immediately to her sister.

"Has something happened to Janet?" she asked as her pulse quickened.

"No . . . nothing like that." He caught hold of her arm as if to steady her.

"I just wanted to talk to you, Eleanor," he added. "So I thought I'd wait here."

Her muscles all seemed to freeze. He let go of her arm while she was enquiring coldly.

"What did you want to say, then?"

He took a step back and turned away from her harsh gaze to indicate his car.

"We could talk on the way," he said uncertainly. "I'm going to collect Janet and drive her to my aunt's house."

Eleanor inclined her head stiffly and led the way to the car. It was only a five-minute run, she told herself. She might as well accept rather than discuss the matter of the pavement here.

Before he started the engine he glanced across at her.

"I miss you, Eleanor," he said. "I miss you a lot."

Keeping her head averted, she made no reply. Her body remained rigid but a storm of emotion was rushing through her mind as she suddenly realised that his words were the echo of her own feelings. She missed him — she missed him desperately.

The she heard him saying in hurt, reproachful tones:

"We were right for each other, Eleanor, and we should never have broken up the way we did."

"No?" A surge of anger shot through her as she accused him. "You were the one who had your eye on someone else! You made it obvious that you were bored with me! You were delighted to be free of me!"

He gave her a swift, astonished glance.

"That's not true," he said.

And after a few seconds had elapsed, he went on, "I'm sorry if that's what you think. But truly, Eleanor, I've never been interested in any other girl since I met you."

She refused to listen to the appeal in his voice.

"But you can't deny that you've been seeing another girl," she said icily.

"No, I don't deny it," he spoke slowly, carefully, "Lynne is a lovely person. She is gentle, kind and considerate, but I've suddenly realised that she doesn't matter to me, it's only *you* I care about.

"I still love you, Eleanor . . . I was hoping you felt the same."

While he was speaking, they reached her home and after he pulled on the handbrake, he looked at her.

"What do you say, Eleanor?"

"Nothing," she replied sharply, "except thanks for the lift. Shall I tell Janet you are here? Or do you want to come in?"

"No — I'll wait here," he answered in heavy, deflated tones.

LATER that evening Eleanor's mother tried to draw her out.

"I wish you'd tell me what's troubling you, Eleanor. You hardly eat a meal these days and you are not sleeping well. Your light was still on at one o'clock this morning."

"I'm OK, Mum. Don't fuss," Eleanor answered with a weak smile.

"Are you still hankering after Keith Cameron?" Mrs Aitken asked gently.

Eleanor shook her head, blushing.

"I've told you. That's all over. I prefer to forget him," she said sharply.

"Well you are behaving like someone in love." Mrs Aitken sighed. "I do wish that the two . . ."

But Eleanor did not wait to hear. She flounced out of the room and hurried upstairs. A few minutes later, she went unwillingly to

In November . . .

THE year is drawing to a close,
   And Earth her misty garments wears.
The chill that heralds winter snows
   Fills the now crisp evening air.
The russet leaves in hedgerows lie,
   Packed tightly by the autumn gales,
While swollen streams flow quickly by,
   Engorged by sudden heavy rains.

Flocks of starlings now are gathering,
   And the now familiar din
Of their shrill insistent calling,
   Sees a pageantry begin.
Small the flocks at first arriving,
   All the afternoon they fly
Like darkening clouds, from hedge and garden,
   Helter-skelter 'cross the sky.

They fill the trees now, row on row,
   Branches bending 'neath the weight,
As quickly now their numbers grow,
   In deafening quarrel, still they wait.
Then suddenly, as by a sign,
   As one, the congregation springs
Into the air, and off in line,
   With thunderous roar of whirring wings.

In thousands now they fill the sky,
   To arc away in splendid chase,
As to the thickets now they fly,
   In loud dispute of roosting space.
Soon all their chattering abates,
   For now the evenings longer grow,
As hushed, and still, the land awaits
   Its blanketing of winter snow.

           — *F. J. Hodgson*

watch from her window as Keith Cameron helped Janet out of his car and escorted her to the front door.

A powerful longing swept over Eleanor as she turned away. But no, she told herself, it's better to forget him. This love business is simply a biological trap. You only have to look at your own sister to realise that people get snared by nature so that the next generation will come into the world.

Be warned, Eleanor told herself sternly, stay clear of any entanglement.

For a moment, she recalled the sadness in Keith's eyes and the sincerity of his voice. But she locked the memories away in her heart. She must steel herself to forget all about Keith Cameron.

In the days that followed, she summoned up all her strength of character to appear outwardly bright and cheerful. Then just as she was beginning to believe that she was happy, her spirits plummeted again.

Her sister had been on the phone and when the call was over her joy was written all over her face.

"George is coming home tomorrow! The contract has gone through a week earlier than he thought. Isn't that marvellous? I can hardly believe it!"

Eleanor nodded and smiled. But there was a terrible hollowness in her mind as she thought . . . what will I do with myself when Janet has gone?

Janet was over the moon. But soon it seemed that the excitement had been too much for her. Then gradually it became obvious that she was in labour.

Eleanor wept as she watched the ambulance driving away.

"Don't worry," Her father patted her shoulder awkwardly. "Your mother is with her . . . she'll be all right."

Brushing away her tears, Eleanor demanded angrily:

"How can you say that when you saw just how much pain she was suffering?"

"She'll forget all that," Mr Aitken answered, "once she has her baby."

But Eleanor could not believe him and in a strained atmosphere they returned to the sitting-room to wait. After a while Mr Aitken fell asleep in his armchair and Eleanor stretched out wearily on the sofa.

Next thing she knew it was ten o'clock in the morning and her mother was beaming with smiles as she handed Eleanor a cup of tea.

"Janet has a son," Mrs Aitken was saying happily. "He weighs six pounds two ounces and he is beautiful."

IN the afternoon Eleanor went to the hospital with flowers for her sister and a floppy teddy-bear for the baby.

Janet was sitting up in bed looking pale and tired but pleased with herself — and immensely proud of her baby, who lay sleeping in her arms.

"He is lovely." Eleanor admired the baby and asked, "What will you call him?"

"I don't know," Janet answered vaguely. "George and I made a list of names we liked . . ." Her voice tapered off into silence as if she had lost interest in the subject.

Eleanor tried for the next few minutes to keep up a flow of conversation but it was difficult when her sister seemed so tired and listless.

Then the door opened and suddenly Janet's face was transformed by a brilliant smile as she greeted her husband.

"George! It's just wonderful. Isn't it just wonderful?"

Eleanor stood up, murmuring an excuse as she made a tactful exit. But she knew that they did not notice. Then as she was about to close the door, she paused for a few seconds to marvel at the radiance which filled the atmosphere.

Mother, father and child were united. They seemed to be in a glorious world of their own.

As she closed the door Eleanor felt a lump in her throat and her eyes were moist. Her vision was blurred and she had to blink to make sure that the man behind her was Keith Cameron.

She knew that he must also have witnessed the touching scene as he said in a husky voice:

"I'll come back later — I met George at the airport and he insisted on bringing me up here to see his son."

Eleanor glanced at the closed door as if her thoughts were reluctant to leave the joy the family inside were sharing.

But now Keith was drawing her away, his hand on her elbow warm and comforting.

She turned towards him as if to speak, yet she had no words. She looked into his eyes and it was as if a great light caught her in its beam.

Keith's arm slid round her waist and they walked together, their steps matching.

In a voice pitched low with emotion Keith said:

"We are together again, aren't we, Eleanor?" And as he sensed a hesitation in her, he told her swiftly:

"You were right, darling, I was to blame for our break-up. I didn't know it at the time but now I realise that I was flattered when someone else made it obvious that she was attracted to me. Maybe I should have had more sense because I knew all along that it's you I love."

He halted and swung her round to face him.

"Forgive me?" he pleaded.

She looked up into his eyes.

"I love you," Eleanor told him softly.

And as their lips met, a shiver of delight tingled through her. She held him close, vowing in her heart that from now on she would never let him go. □

THERE was a new topic of conversation in Kinroddie — the local flying club were busy organising their first-ever air show.

Planes would be flying in from other clubs for the great day and there would be pleasure flights, aerial acrobatics, and lots more.

I had a passing interest in the event, nothing more, because of my boyfriend, who didn't seem all that keen either. This surprised me because Mike Rankine was an engineer, and usually interested in all things mechanical.

That's why being asked to take part in the air show came as a complete surprise and it happened a few weeks before.

One evening, Mike and I were in the golf clubhouse and as usual he was analysing his round shot by shot. It irritated me — as far as I was concerned when something was finished, it was completely over and done with.

Mike had just reached his approach shot to the fifteenth green when Doug Royce approached our table, pulled up a chair and sat down.

"I'm about to add a touch of excitement to your lives." He grinned. "As you know, I'm on the organising committee for the air show. I'm looking for two volunteers to do a parachute jump for charity."

"A parachute jump," Mike echoed. "Just like that."

"Of course not 'just like that,'" Doug explained. "You'd be given a crash training course in jumping."

"That's a comfort," Mike said, a hint of sarcasm in his voice.

"Now, don't be like that," Doug said breezily, with a broad sweep

by JOAN DOUGLAS

152

of his arm. "Think of yourselves, Kinroddie's most eligible young couple leaping from a plane at five thousand feet. I can see you now drifting downwards together. It's almost romantic."

"Sorry, you'll have to find someone else," Mike said.

"What a shame." Doug sighed. "And it's for charity, too. I've sounded out everyone in the golf club and they're willing to sponsor your jump."

Doug turned to me.

"Elaine, can't you talk him into it?"

"No she can't," Mike said sharply. "Anyway, she wouldn't dream of jumping either."

With Mike, I usually kept quiet or agreed. This time I agreed.

As we were driving home he became quite scathing about Doug Royce.

"Of all the nerve, asking us to perform a stunt like that."

Strange that Doug had touched on one of those hidden ambitions never likely to be achieved which is why they're so appealing.

"I think it might have been fun," I replied.

"Don't tell me you were thinking about it?"

"As a matter of fact I was."

"But that's not for you?"

"Why not?"

"Well, you're just a slip of a girl. I'd hate to think of you . . ."

"I'm not just a 'slip of a girl,' there's more to me than just the way I look," I replied hotly. "And if you must know, I've always wanted to do something exciting like that."

"But you won't, will you?"

When Mike tried to put me off things, I always felt rebellious and hit back.

"You were quick to refuse. Surely you weren't scared?"

"Me, scared!" he said in astonishment. "Of course not. In fact, I was quite tempted to take up Doug's offer."

"Why didn't you?"

"Concern for you. I didn't think you'd like me doing something dangerous. It wouldn't have been fair to have you worrying about me."

When Mike spoke like that in such caring terms I was easily won over.

Mike took me in his arms long enough to make me forget the nagging doubts I harboured about our relationship.

THAT night before going to bed I took a long glance at myself in the mirror. I saw a small slender girl with a serious oval face, bluey-green eyes, a small straight nose and curved mouth.

My hair was the colour of autumn leaves brushed back in gentle waves.

Yet my reflection told me nothing I wanted to know. I was nineteen with little experience of life, while Mike was wordly at twenty-two, and so different from my previous boyfriend.

Anything You Can Do!

Jack Gray was a reporter on the local paper and we'd known each other since childhood.

Perhaps it was this familiarity which forced us to drift apart, both seeking something different now we were adults. With Jack it was his job; with me, some more exploring life, and I found that stimulation in Mike's company.

At first our friendship was great. I was content to follow faithfully in Mike's shadow, never questioning his making decisions for us both — until people hinted that we might not be right for each other.

We certainly were poles apart. Mike was so super confident, while I was so quiet, until the doubts built up in my mind, too. But I comforted myself knowing that many of those sneering at us were former girlfriends of Mike's, whom he'd long ago discarded and were probably jealous of my position.

I'd have forgotten the charity parachute jump altogether if a rather sharp-nosed local reporter hadn't reminded me.

I was having my lunch break from the insurance office where I worked when Jack Gray found me in the park.

"The very person I'm looking for," he said triumphantly. "My sources tell me you might be doing a parachute jump at the air show."

"Well, you can put your notebook away," I said sharply. "I've no intention of doing any such thing."

I laughed at his nonplussed expression.

"I was thinking about having a go until Mike talked me out of it. He was very concerned."

"Doesn't sound like the Mike Rankine I know," Jack said thoughtfully.

"And what's that supposed to mean?" I bristled.

"You know, too full of his own importance to think of anyone else."

Snide remarks about Mike often made me back him up. I suppose it was a kind of defence mechanism to eliminate any doubts in my mind about our relationship.

"If you must know, Mike was very concerned, unselfish, too. Though he wanted to jump himself he refused, thinking I might be worried about him doing something so dangerous."

"Sounds like you just let him dominate your life. Does he make all your decisions for you?"

"No, he doesn't," I replied crossly. "And you're just saying that to annoy me. You didn't like my taking up with Mike so you're trying to get your own back."

Jack shook his head.

"You're wrong, Elaine. All I was thinking was that if you really want to do that parachute jump, go ahead and do it — Mike or no Mike."

"Just so you can have a story for the paper, I suppose?"

"Not at all." Jack smiled. "I still have an interest in you, remember? I'd like to see you getting what you want out of life."

155

"I don't believe you, Jack Gray. You're just trying to drive a wedge between Mike and me."

"Think that if you like." Jack sighed.

"That's exactly what I do think," I said, storming off.

Tears stung my eyes, my mood was a mixture of anger and bewilderment. Jack wasn't a vindictive person, yet I was uncertain of his motive in suggesting I went through with the parachute jump.

Was it really concern for me or was he after a good newspaper story?

I was in an agony of uncertainty until I met Mike that evening.

Then as I waited for him in the hotel lounge I knew exactly what I was going to suggest . . .

YOU look excited about something?" asked Mike.

"I am," I replied with a smile. "About what we decided about not doing the parachuting. Let's change our minds, it'll be good fun. *And* Jack Gray will give us a good write-up in the paper. We might even be photographed.

"We'll have proper training," I rushed on, "so the risk will be lessened, and it is for charity."

"No, I'd rather not."

"But I don't understand. You like a challenge like that."

"I've said no, haven't I?"

"Can I have a reason?"

"I just don't want to, that's my reason."

By the way Mike turned his gaze from me, I knew his refusal went deeper than that.

"Please, Mike . . ." I pleaded.

His eyes flickered uncertainly, something I'd never seen before.

"If you must know, I'm terrified of flying, always have been." His reaction was to glare fiercely at me. "There now, are you satisfied?"

It was all becoming clearer to me now. Mike, the great outdoors man, into every sport, yet the only activity he didn't take part in was the flying club.

"There's nothing to be ashamed of, Mike. Everyone has a phobia of some sort."

He half-smiled. "Thanks for being so understanding."

"Isn't that what friends are for?" I replied. "Look, Mike, I've something to ask you."

"What is it?"

"I appreciate your concern in not wanting me to jump, but I think I'd like to have a go. High time I achieved something in life. You wouldn't mind, would you?"

His face became a study in anxiety.

"Why not, it's *my* life, Mike."

I was surprised by his reaction.

"Go on then," he said dismissively, "jump if you like, don't think about me."

"You?" I echoed. "I don't understand."

"What's everyone going to think when they see me being beaten by a slip of a girl?"

I simply couldn't believe what I was hearing.

"Is that all you're worried about, your image? Don't my feelings count?" I demanded. "And I thought you cared, the other night when you were so concerned about me . . ."

I felt my heart sinking as the truth began to dawn.

"Or perhaps you were just concerned for yourself when you talked me out of jumping. Were you, Mike?"

He looked at me shamefacedly.

"Yes, I was."

I replied with a controlled anger.

"You should have told me the truth the other night instead of lying about your concern for me, that I can't forgive. As for your image, there isn't much of it left when I think how you tried to hide behind my skirt.

"I thought two people should be able to trust each other, Mike. Obviously my idea of friendship differs from yours.

"Well I've news for you. This 'slip of a girl' as you like to call me, won't be around any more to amuse you and boost your ego. From now on I'm going to start leading my own life — and I'm beginning at the air show."

There was a sneer in Mike's voice.

"You won't jump. You haven't got the courage."

"Then I suggest you turn up at the air show and find out."

That was the moment I turned my back on Mike and walked out of his life.

ONLY when I started my crash course did I wonder what I'd really let myself in for. So many things to learn . . . leaving the plane, when to open the 'chute, how to land.

I might have given up had it not been for the promised charitable donations and my pride, too, of course. Most importantly, here was my first real chance to prove myself as a person in my own right, not living in Mike's shadow.

At last the big day arrived and I was only vaguely aware of Doug Royce helping me into the plane where I sat miserably on the floor. Seats had been removed to make room for the parachutists and their equipment.

Is it worth it, I asked myself miserably, as we lifted into the sky. Because of this jump I'd lost Mike. Jack, too, probably, after the way I shouted at him in the park.

I glanced from the window and shivered at the postage-stamp-size air strip far below. How will I ever land on there, I asked myself panic-stricken.

Only when Doug turned his head from the pilot's seat to speak did my training take over.

"You can still change your mind, Elaine, no-one will think any the less of you."

"*I'll* think a lot less of me," I shouted above the noise of the engines.

I'm sure it was just his way of making me more determined, for he grinned widely at me.

"Better get ready then, five minutes to go. There's very little wind so you shouldn't have any difficulty."

This was the worst part of all, on hands and knees crawling out of the door backwards, to grasp the wing struts, place feet on the wheel. Done it so often on the ground but at five thousand feet with the slipstream tearing at me . . .

Must thank Doug for slowing the plane down . . . made it . . . hanging on like grim death . . . I must be mad . . . could be out shopping as usual. Waiting for Doug's signal . . . must be exact or I'll miss the airfield.

Doug's signal now . . . throw myself backwards . . . dropping like a stone . . . plane getting smaller. Counting the numbers until release . . . *now!*

Panic . . . nothing's happening . . . I'm still falling. Sudden jerk upwards . . . parachute open . . . floating down.

No time to admire the scenery . . . work to do. Ground coming up fast . . . pull guide lines turning myself into the wind . . . will I land correctly?

A jarring sensation . . . roll over to break the fall . . . on the ground at last, parachute falling round me like a shroud. Still alive, I think. Feeling for broken bones . . . none . . . elation, I've done it!

Gentle hands releasing me from my harness . . . showers of congratulations.

On my feet again now and there's someone there I hadn't expected to see.

"What are you doing here?" I asked, knowing all the time.

Jack smiled. "Miss Milne, what are your immediate reactions to your experience?"

"Glad to be alive, I felt so fragile up there. So many regrets that I hadn't done anything with my life." Suddenly the little things seemed important like patching up differences with an old friend. I heard myself saying with a choke in my voice, "We've always been friends, haven't we, Jack?"

"You could say that," he replied with that disarming smile of his.

Suddenly I felt ashamed. In my desire to find status among Mike's circle of friends I'd overlooked Jack, always around when I needed him for my bad times during schooldays and since.

He smiled. "There's a perfect spot I know for mending friendships, along by the river bank. How about this evening?"

"Just perfect." I smiled. "That is, if you don't mind being seen with just a slip of a girl."

"Not at all," came his reply, and by the look in his eyes I knew he meant it. □

Ruined Castle

THE castle glooms on the hilltop high,
    Partly enshrouded by whispering
    trees
Whose leaves a-tremble give a soft
    sigh,
    Surging gently on breathing breeze.

And far below the sea rolls in glee,
    Filling the rock-bestrewn bay,
The fishing boats glide in from the sea,
    Birds are circling in glad array.

The crumbling walls and turreted roof
    Shine forth 'neath the westering sun
Proclaiming in silence, historical proof,
    Bearing beauty from ages won.
               — *Margaret Comer.*

The Things

That Matter Most!

by GILLIAN FRASER

OLD Alec Murray raised his head from the pillow as he heard his granddaughter's quiet footsteps on the stairs.

"Eileen's home," he whispered to his wife, Sarah.

"Then perhaps you'll stop worrying and go to sleep," she chided gently, but really just as relieved as Alec to have the girl safely back home again.

She snuggled into his side. "Put the light out, Alec."

Though the darkness was restful, sleep escaped him. Alec lay on his back staring at the darkened ceiling.

Sarah slid her hand into his. "Alec, can you not stop brooding?"

"You know I can't sleep these nights, lass," he replied.

Sarah sighed. "You and that theatre. Can't you accept the inevitable that it's to be domolished?"

"Never," Alec growled.

"I'm proud of you, Alec. Nobody's fought harder than you to save it. But the decision's been made."

But Alec's mind was in a turmoil. He just couldn't make any sense out of the decision to destroy a fine old building like the Dominion Theatre, and put in its place some monstrosity of a modern office block.

His mind slipped back to the halcyon days when the Dominion had been at its peak, packed to capacity every night with enthusiastic audiences. Nothing could dim the magic of Music Hall, he thought, remembering vividly the excitement of each new show — and the part he'd played in so many.

Alec wasn't a performer, but as far as he was concerned, his job had been much grander. How proud he'd been of his commissionaire's green uniform with epaulettes, shiny buttons and peaked cap.

Of course, he hadn't started as a commissionaire, but a stage hand. As the years passed, Alec prided himself that there wasn't a job in the theatre he couldn't do. Many of the famous Music Hall artistes

L

who'd performed at the Dominion had become personal friends.

Yet Alec had always gazed admiringly at that fine green uniform worn then by big John Dodds as he scrutinised the tickets at the door. The two had become friends; and John, who was nearing retirement, dazzled the younger man with stories about theatre life.

John would draw deeply on his pipe and utter the words which had followed Alec down the years,

"There's no place quite like the Old Dominion."

To Alec there was no person quite like John Dodds, for when John retired, he put in a good word for Alec to take his place. All those years ago, Alec reminisced. Now the well-worn green uniform hung upstairs in what Alec called his "Trophy Room."

Conscious of Sarah sleeping beside him and Eileen padding about in the next room, he realised that life had its compensations. How quickly young Eileen — so cruelly robbed of her parents in a boating accident — had blossomed into a lovely young woman. He and Sarah were pleased, too, that there was a young man in her life, and quite dependable, so they'd heard.

A S twenty-year-old Eileen prepared for bed, she felt she was the luckiest girl in the world. On her arrival home, she had wanted desperately to rush into her grandparents' room and tell them the exciting news, but decided to wait till morning.

Snuggling down between the sheets, she felt quite dizzy with excitement at the thought of her handsome young architect. I don't believe it, she told herself. I've only met him twice, and now . . .

"Well, I never," Gran exclaimed, when Eileen told her. "He's asked you to a dance."

"Not only that, Gran. But he's coming to the house here to collect me, so you and Grandpa will be able to meet him."

Alec looked questioningly at Eileen over his specs.

"This young architect of yours, he's not by any chance connected with the new office block scheme."

"Of course not," she replied, then added as if doubtful, "at least, I don't think so."

▶p164

THERE'S no doubt that the windmill at Rye in Sussex is an impressive building. There has been a mill on this site since the 1720s, though the present structure is just over fifty years old. It replaced a mill that was destroyed by fire, and later it saw "active service" when it was commandeered by the Army as a lookout during the war. The town of Rye is a charming place with lots of "character" to be found in the cobbled streets and attractive houses. To the east are the misty Romney Marshes, once a favourite haunt of smugglers.

THE WINDMILL, RYE, SUSSEX : J CAMPBELL KERR

"Really, Alec," Sarah scolded. "There are dozens of architects in Glenmuir. Why should Gordon have any connection?"

Alec was about to launch into another of his "Save the Dominion" tirades, when a look from Sarah stopped him. Alec glanced at Eileen in time to see an almost hurt look in her eye. He smiled.

"I'm sure Gordon wouldn't have any connection with a scheme like that," he said.

But Eileen felt apprehensive. Naturally where Gordon worked had never crossed her mind. What difference does it make anyway, she assured herself.

"You must ask Gordon to tea, dear," Sarah suggested. "Then you can go on to the dance."

"A good idea,," Alec said, winking. "Then we can decide whether or not we approve of him."

"Stop teasing, Alec," Sarah scolded. She turned to Eileen. "Tell Gordon he's very welcome."

Sarah hugged her grandparents.

"You're both wonderful," she said happily.

★   ★   ★   ★

As the day of the dance arrived, her excitement was tempered with a slight fear. Why, she asked herself. Was it because more than anything else she wanted her wonderful grandparents who'd devoted their lives to her, to approve of Gordon?

A sense of frustration swept over her. Meeting Gordon, life had suddenly taken on a new meaning, and now so soon, she was beset with doubt. With Grandpa's attitude to the theatre project and architects in general, she felt concerned that Gordon was coming to the house on trial.

Yet when he looked so self-assured coming up the garden path, she began to feel that if anyone could stand up to Grandfather's brusque manner, he could.

"Meet Gordon," she told her grandparents proudly.

Though outwardly calm, her heart was thumping uncomfortably. She wanted their first meeting to be a happy one.

"We're always pleased to meet Eileen's friends, aren't we, Alec?" Sarah said.

The old man shook hands with Gordon.

"Of course, we don't know much about you," he said bluntly, but added, smiling, "what we've heard is good."

"Thanks, Mr Murray," Gordon replied modestly. "There isn't all that much to know about me really."

Alec gave the young man an appraising look. Good firm handshake and steady gaze, he noted. Confident that Gordon would be able to handle himself in a crisis, he was favourably impressed.

"Come and sit down, Gordon," he invited. "You and I'll have a wee chat while the lassies make the tea."

Eileen felt herself on tenterhooks as she journeyed to and from the kitchen. Much to her relief, the two men seemed to be getting on fine. At last the tea was on the table helping to bridge that first awkward gap.

"Your baking is delicious, Mrs Murray," the young man complimented.

Sarah's eye caught Eileen's in a gesture of approval, for which the younger girl was very thankful. Her grandmother was the perfect hostess, shaping the conversation, passing it round, yet shielding Gordon from too many of Alec's pointed questions.

WHEN tea was over, Sarah made a suggestion.

"Alec, you take Gordon upstairs and show him your Trophy Room."

Gordon followed Alec upstairs.

"Has Eileen mentioned this?" the old man asked.

"She did mention something about it," Gordon replied.

Alec opened a door. "Here we are then, Gordon. This is what I call my Trophy Room."

The room was full from floor to ceiling with theatrical souvenirs. Gordon gasped and Alec laughed.

"Ay, it surprises most people."

There were programmes by the thousand. Stage props were stacked in boxes as well as files full of old Music Hall songs. Another shelf

▶*over*

they were first...

IT was for her work in radioactivity that Marie Curie was the first woman to be awarded the Nobel Prize for Physics — an honour she shared with her husband in 1903.

Polish-born Marie worked exclusively in France, and won a second Nobel Prize — this time for Chemistry — in 1911. She eventually died of leukaemia, brought on by her close contact with radioactive materials.

contained autograph books filled with the names of famous Music Hall artistes. Photos of the famous and not so famous adorned the walls and ceiling.

"I've heard my father mention some of these names," Gordon said.

As the old man weaved his tales about the great days of Music Hall, Gordon found himself caught up in the spell. He felt the expectancy of "Curtain Up," heard the Overture.

Alec talked about people, clothed them and made them real.

Suddenly, Gordon felt privileged to know a man lke Alec Murray. Here was a man who believed in fighting for what was right, no matter how much pain and anguish it cost him.

"I suppose as an architect, you know what's happening to the Dominion Theatre?" Alec said finally.

The younger man nodded.

"It's stood a hundred years," Alec protested. "Now it's to go, to make way for one of these awful modern office blocks."

Suddenly he clapped the young man on the shoulder. "Pay no attention to me, Gordon. That's just the rumblings of a disillusioned old man." He smiled. "It's not as if that project's your concern anyway.

"Still," he went on, "I'd be glad of your opinion, as an outside observer, of course."

"I've seen the plans," Gordon told him. "I can assure you the new building will not be ugly. The design will be such that the new structure will blend with the older surroundings."

Gordon was suddenly surprised to find himself echoing the words of Sam Docherty, words that he had once agreed with. Now however, having seen Alec Murray's love for the old theatre, he felt more than ever at variance with Sam Docherty's ideas.

But what can I do against the head of the firm, he thought miserably.

Alec looked at him suspiciously. "You seem to know a lot about this theatre project."

Gordon took a deep breath.

"I happen to work for Docherty's, the architects. We're designing the new block."

A look of pain crossed Alec's face.

"I see," he whispered hoarsely. "I should have known you'd be one of them."

"I don't understand, Mr Murray. One of what?"

"One of those architects destroying the theatre!" the old man exclaimed angrily.

Gordon knew he should've been more tactful knowing now how much the theatre meant to the older man, but on the other hand . . .

"If I've offended you in any way, I certainly didn't mean to, but you did ask my opinion," he said.

Alec made to say something, but Gordon stopped him.

"Please hear me out, Mr Murray. I see the Dominion as a fine building. We've looked at ways of preserving it, even down to building the block as a theatre extension. We are human, you know, but we have to be practical.

"No-one wants a theatre in Glenmuir, and the theatre has been up for sale for two years now. Much better to use the space for an office block which can bring work to the town."

Despite Alec's intransigence he was open minded enough to admit himself that Gordon could be right. Anyway, he found himself respecting the young man for his firm opinions and the way he'd put them over. Yet he was in a quandary.

He loved Eileen dearly and wanted her happiness. If Gordon were to be her choice would he not always be a reminder of those who'd destroyed his beloved theatre?

"We'd better go back downstairs," he retorted flatly.

WERE you impressed then, Gordon?" Sarah asked.
"Very much so," the young man replied.

Alec looked pointedly at Eileen. "You didn't tell me Gordon worked for the firm of architects who are designing the new office block."

Eileen's face registered a mixture of shock and alarm. "I didn't know."

"Blame me," Gordon explained. "When Eileen told me of your love for the theatre I should have mentioned my involvement."

"Nonsense," Sarah retorted. "Alec Murray," she scolded. "Of all the things to fuss over. Eileen and Gordon are only interested in each other, and quite rightly, too."

Alec's mind was suddenly filled with memories of his own courting days, when he too had no time for anyone but the hazel-eyed daughter of the head gardener at the manor. Thoughts came of those sweet kisses beneath the cool of the tall cypress trees, the heady fragrance of roses in full bloom.

Yet still his nostalgia was dulled in an onrush of bitterness — realising that all he'd stood for in his life was coming down with the theatre.

Despite Sarah's attempt to keep the atmosphere relaxed, the conversation had become tense and strained.

The young people should have been pleased to escape to the excitement of the dance, but the atmosphere of doubt seemed to have followed them as they sat later at the side of the dance floor sipping cooling drinks.

"I should've told you," Gordon said.

Eileen didn't seem to have heard for she was too busy thinking about her grandfather.

"Grandpa was hurt, wasn't he?" she queried.

"He was, but he'll get over it."

"Oh, you make it sound all so easy," she retorted. "Will he? After all, he's a proud man — and devoted to the Dominion."

"Don't you think I know that?" replied Gordon crossly. "I saw his

Trophy Room, remember? I tried to explain we'd loked at all ways of preserving the place."

There was a tense pause before Gordon exclaimed, "I don't know why *I* should be feeling guilty about anything. I'm only doing my job, after all."

"Is that all that matters to you, Gordon?"

"I didn't mean it like that. Why do you pick me up wrongly . . . ?" His voice tailed off miserably, there was little else to say, the evening was in ruins.

"Take me home, please, Gordon," Eileen said coolly.

"Can't we start again, they're playing a waltz?" Gordon suggested.

But they were stiff and unyielding in each other's arms and left the dance floor halfway through.

The car journey home was miserable. An impenetrable barrier had somehow become erected between them.

"Stay and talk to me for a few minutes," Gordon pleaded desperately, as Eileen opened the car door.

"I'd rather not," she replied. "Good night, Gordon."

ALEC and Sarah were surprised to see her home so early. Even more surprised when she rushed past them up the stairs into her room and banged the door. Sarah made to follow her, but Alec laid a restraining hand on her arm.

"Leave her, lass. Whatever's the matter, it's between her and Gordon."

Sarah looked meaningly at her husband. "Can you really be certain of that, Alec Murray?"

Eileen threw herself down on the bed. Tears of anguish poured down her cheeks as the full realisation of what had happened hit her. Have I lost Gordon for ever, she wondered. Will I ever see him again?

It seemed a long time later when Sarah came into the room, cradled the girl's head in her arms and gently stroked her hair. As the hurt dissolved from her, Eileen poured out her heart.

"What am I going to do, Gran? I love Gordon, but I love Grandpa as well. If Gordon and I see each other again, Grandpa will be so hurt. I don't want that. I'd rather give up Gordon first."

Sarah felt deeply for Eileen.

"Och, lassie!" the older woman exclaimed. "You don't know your grandpa awfully well, do you? He'd never want you to sacrifice your future happiness, just because he has strong opinions about things. Gordon has also, and your grandfather respects him for that."

"Does he?" Eileen asked. She put her arms round her grandmother. "I seem to have made a mess of everything. Here was I, convinced I'd made the big sacrifice tonight walking out on Gordon, and now —"

Suddenly she felt panic stricken. "What am I going to do, Gran? What if Gordon won't see me again? I couldn't blame him, really, if he didn't want to."

The Things That Matter Most

After dropping Eileen, Gordon returned to his tiny flat. He didn't feel hurt, just bewildered at their sudden reversal in fortunes. He loved Eileen and didn't doubt that their love, despite difficulties, would grow and blossom.

He thought about Alec Murray and felt nothing but admiration for a man who would fight so hard for what he believed in.

Gordon looked despondently at his drawing board with its jumble of half-finished sketches. He'd spent so long on this theatre project it had almost become an obsession with him, yet he'd never been able to come up with a way of saving the theatre and possibly incorporating it into the new office block.

"You come up with an idea and it'll be considered," his boss, Sam Docherty, had told him.

Gordon had come up with dozens, but there was no way structurally that the new block could be grafted on to the existing theatre building.

Gordon sat looking at the blank sheet of paper before him for ages and ages. Having met Alec Murray, he was more than ever convinced that something of the Dominion should be preserved. He could still see the pride on the old man's face as he'd displayed the contents and treasures of his Trophy Room.

Gordon's hand flew to his mouth in amazement, his heart raced.

"Of course, that's it!" He gasped excitedly. Suddenly, everything became clear.

That night, he sat long at his drawing board, sketching, altering, making scribbled calculations. At last, when he finally made his way to bed in the early hours of the morning, a feeling of excitement kept sleep from him.

He was sure his plan would work, but would Sam Docherty like it? It *has* to work, he thought desperately, for Eileen and myself — but more importantly, Alec Murray.

DESPITE the inevitability of the theatre demolition, Alec still devoted himself daily in his temporary job as caretaker to keeping the Dominion spick and span. He enjoyed his daily visits. They kept him in touch with memories of years gone by.

Though alone in the dark vault of an empty and lifeless theatre, Alec didn't mind at all, for the place was part of him, like an extra skin. But today he felt more miserable than ever before. He was terribly conscious that his devotion to the Dominion was having a traumatic effect on his family.

I never wanted that, he thought desperately, hoping that something might still turn up to save the theatre.

"Are you Alec Murray?"

Alone with his thoughts, Alec hadn't noticed the stranger walking down the aisle towards the stage.

"That's me," he replied, adding tersely, "The theatre's closed."

"I'd like to come on the stage," the man asked, "just to have a look at the theatre?"

Alec shrugged his shoulders indifferently. "Help yourself."

The stranger climbed the steps, walking purposefully towards him. He gazed out across the empty auditorium.

"Very impressive, very impressive indeed," he said.

"I suppose you know the theatre's being pulled down?" Alec asked.

"Yes, and I suppose like me you're sad to see it."

"Heartbroken's more the word," Alec retorted. "A hundred years of history being reduced to rubble. It's just not fair."

"I'm afraid I don't know much of the history. Why don't you tell me?" the stranger asked.

As he became caught up in Alec's story-telling, the empty theatre seemed to light up for the older man. The theatre was crowded. There was spectacle, music and laughter. Before him trooped an endless entertainment of acrobats, magicians, singers, comedians, just

▶p172

TUCKED into the rugged Fife coastline, the royal burgh of Pittenweem is truly a picturesque spot. The village grew up around an ancient 12th-century priory — the remains of which can still be seen. With its beautifully-restored houses in the narrow streets around the harbour, Pittenweem today is an artist's delight, but it should also be remembered that the same lovely harbour is an important source of income for the village. It's from there that the fishing boats sail out past the Isle of May to the North Sea in search of their catches. There surely can be no livelier sight than when the boats return to unload, and the waterfront becomes a hive of activity.

PITTENWEEM, Fife : J CAMPBELL KERR

as he'd seen them all those years ago when his parents had taken him.

"I'd almost forgotten," the stranger said.

"I can never forget," Alec said.

"Now I can understand why you love this place," the stranger sympathised. He realised not only had he been witnessing the love of Alec Murray for his theatre, but he — Sam Docherty — was mourning the passing of the great age of Music Hall.

As he had listened to Alec Murray, for a while the pressures of business had fallen from his shoulders, and Sam felt better for it.

"Sorry," Alec muttered. "When I'm talking about the Old Dominion, I get rather carried away."

"Glad you did," the stranger said. "Now I know the quality of the man who's been giving my planning office a few headaches."

"Planning office?" Alec queried.

"Let me introduce myself. I'm Sam Docherty, Managing Director of the firm building the new office complex."

Alec was angry. "I should've guessed who you were. Now you've had your laugh, perhaps you'd better go."

"I didn't come to laugh, Mr Murray. I'm here for a very serious purpose. "Let me explain. Up to a short time ago, our plans were firm, then one of my bright young architects came to me with an idea which I'm sure you'll approve of. Obviously, of course, you'll understand that it's nothing to do with retaining the theatre as a complete unit. That's just not possible."

His eyes twinkled. "I believe you know the young man in question, Gordon Finlay?"

"Ay," Alec said. "He and my granddaughter are very friendly."

"So he'd led me to understand," Sam replied. "Gordon Finlay's a fine young man. I like to see my employees well settled in life. Perhaps we'll hear wedding bells some day?"

Alec felt a rush of guilt. He knew if it hadn't been for his own pig-headedness, there would have been no estrangement between them.

"Well, I'm not sure about that," he replied.

"But to my suggestion," Sam said urgently. "I'd like you to come to my office for a while. There's something that will interest you very much."

He paused to allow what he'd said to take root in Alec's mind. "My car's waiting outside to take you there."

Alec wondered what to do. There was something trustworthy about Sam Docherty. This plus Alec's natural curiosity helped to make his decision.

"Right then," he replied.

AS the two men walked round the office, Sam explained the technicalities of architecture.

"I never realised it was so complicated!" Alec gasped.

"Our job isn't easy. Now take a look at this," Sam said.

They stopped in front of a large table from which Sam removed a dust sheet. Alec saw in front of him a large scale model of the new office complex. He shuddered at its clinical and uninspiring lines.

"You don't like it — obviously," Sam stated.

"No."

"Then come and look at this." He beckoned Alec to another table. As Alec saw what was before him, his heart began to beat faster.

"Well, what d'you think about it?" Sam asked.

What was laid out before Alec was what appeared to be the plan of some kind of museum.

"I still don't quite understand," he said.

"Ah," Sam said. "Here's Mr Finlay now, with your granddaughter, right on cue." Sam smiled. "I'll let him explain, as he designed it. I'm sorry, I'll have to go. I've an important appointment."

He shook Alec's hand. "A privilege to meet you, Mr Murray, and promise me something. Will you show me your Trophy Room sometime?"

"Delighted," Alec replied.

He turned to Eileen. "But what are you doing here? I thought that you and Gordon had, er . . ."

Gordon's laugh interrupted him. "That was just a silly little misunderstanding. This is the real reason we're here." He pointed at the model. "A full-size theatrical museum taking up the ground floor of the office block, with show cases of all your theatrical souvenirs. Now listen to this.

"The main showpiece would be a replica of the Number One Dressing Room as it was in the Twenties with the original material and furniture restored."

"And it was all Gordon's work," Eileen said proudly. "After we quarrelled on the night of the dance, Gordon sat up till the early hours and worked this out. Isn't he wonderful?"

Alec looked at the young couple, unable to hide the tear in his eye. They looked so happy.

"By the way," Gordon added, "a curator will be needed for the museum. We've decided the job's yours, if you want it. And there's one more thing. The new building's to be called The Dominion Complex."

Alec walked home in a daze. Eileen and Gordon were together again, and something of the old theatre was to remain after all. His cup of happiness was complete. He smiled to himself.

As Alec passed the theatre he looked up. Across the span of the years he could hear the booming voice of big John Dodds again.

"Ay, Alec, there's no place quite like the Old Dominion." □

ISBN 0-85116-431-5